DEVELOPMENTAL PSYCHOLOGY FOR THE HEALTH CARE PROFESSIONS

Part 2
Adulthood and Aging

BEHAVIORAL SCIENCES
FOR HEALTH CARE PROFESSIONALS
Michael A. Counte, Series Editor

During the 1970s there was rapid growth in the amount of behavioral science instruction included in the training of physicians, nurses, dentists, pharmacists, and other health care professionals. New faculty members were put on staffs at medical centers, curricula were devised, and on occasion, new departments were created to support a diverse group of behavioral scientists.

The new emphasis on behavioral science in the education of health care professionals and the inclusion of a behavioral science section in certification examinations have generated a need for clinically relevant text materials. This series responds to that need by providing general, yet concise, introductions to common topical areas in behavioral science curricula, linking concepts and theories to clinical practice.

The authors of the series volumes are behavioral scientists with considerable experience in the education of health care professionals. Most of them are also clinicians, and their varied experience enables them to present their topics in a readable fashion. The content of the texts presumes only a very basic knowledge of the behavioral sciences, and emphasis is placed on the practical implications of research findings for health care delivery.

It is our hope that this multivolume approach will allow each instructor to select the books most pertinent to his or her particular curriculum. The division of topics was planned to enhance the overall flexibility of the information being presented.

Titles in This Series

Also of Interest

† Available in hardcover and paperback.

DEVELOPMENTAL PSYCHOLOGY FOR THE HEALTH CARE PROFESSIONS: PART 2 – ADULTHOOD AND AGING

Howard S. Feldman, Ph.D., and Martita A. Lopez, Ph.D.

Rush Medical College

The second in a two-volume set on developmental psychology, this book explores normal psychological development in adulthood and aging. In the past it was thought that life after age 18 was a developmentally static period characterized mainly by decline. The recent dramatic expansion of interest in and research on adulthood and aging has begun to reveal instead the depth and richness of adult development. The authors review major research in this area with a special focus on how psychological, social, and biological changes are related to health and health care.

The text explores such issues as sexuality, marriage, parenthood, and career choice, as well as the effects of work and family life on life stress and illness. In addition to examining the changes that occur in old age and relating those changes to health care, the authors go on to consider the psychological aspects of death and dying, thus completing the life-cycle discussion begun in Part 1.

Howard S. Feldman and *Martita A. Lopez* are assistant professors in the Department of Psychology and Social Sciences at Rush Medical College in Chicago. Dr. Lopez also works extensively in the Johnston R. Bowman Health Center for the Elderly. Dr. Feldman is director of the Office of Behavioral Studies at Rush–Presbyterian–St. Luke's Medical Center.

To our parents

DEVELOPMENTAL PSYCHOLOGY FOR THE HEALTH CARE PROFESSIONS

Part 2
Adulthood and Aging

Howard S. Feldman, Ph.D.
Martita A. Lopez, Ph.D.

Rush Medical College

Westview Press / Boulder, Colorado

Behavioral Sciences for Health Care Professionals

Copyright © 1982 by Westview Press, Inc.

Published in 1982 in the United States of America by
  Westview Press, Inc.
  5500 Central Avenue
  Boulder, Colorado 80301
  Frederick A. Praeger, President and Publisher

Library of Congress Cataloging in Publication Data
Main entry under title:
Developmental psychology for the health care professions.
  (Behavioral sciences for health care professionals)
  Includes bibliographical references and indexes.
  Contents: pt. 1. Prenatal through adolescent development / Katherine A. Billingham—pt. 2. Adulthood and aging / Howard S. Feldman, Martita A. Lopez.
  1. Developmental psychology. I. Billingham, Katherine A. II. Feldman, Howard S. III. Lopez, Martita A. IV. Series. [DNLM: 1. Human development. BF 713 F312]
  BF713.B54 1982   155'.02461   81-16012
  ISBN 0-86531-000-9 (v. 1)   AACR2
  ISBN 0-86531-001-7 (pbk.: v. 1)
  ISBN 0-86531-012-2 (v. 2)
  ISBN 0-86531-013-0 (pbk.: v. 2)

Printed and bound in the United States of America

CONTENTS

TABLES AND FIGURES

1

A DEVELOPMENTAL PERSPECTIVE ON ADULTHOOD

INTRODUCTION

Since the 1960s, there has been growing interest in and research on the adult years of the life cycle. Previously, developmental studies had focused on childhood and adolescence, in which an orderly relationship between age and growth was assumed. Adulthood had been looked at as a time of stability, the end point of earlier developmental processes. The changes presumed to occur during adulthood were typically seen as centering around issues of deterioration that take place gradually, universally, and in an age-related pattern. These assumptions are now being challenged, and the span of time between early adulthood and ultimate death has become an area of great research activity. The new orientation looks at human development as a life-long process with change taking place throughout every phase, and its goal is to identify which changes take place at which points in the life course and to establish the nature of the patterns and interrelationships of these changes. Throughout adulthood, individuals experience growth, stability, stagnation, and deterioration in many aspects of their lives. These processes are subject to an intricate interaction between biological, psychological, and socioenvironmental factors.

We will be looking at three periods of adulthood identified on the basis of chronological age: young adulthood, from 18 to 40; middle adulthood, from 40 to 65; and later adulthood, from 65 until death. This division is somewhat arbitrary, although it has heuristic value; issues and events actually overlap these periods and may occur repeatedly throughout adulthood. The first chapter provides a general overview of adult developmental psychology and explores physiological changes in young and middle adulthood. The second and third chapters explore young and middle adulthood, respectively, and examine psychological issues that are dealt with during those periods, as well as the adult's involvement in relationships and work. The next three chapters focus on later adulthood, with the fourth looking at the relationship between health and aging and the fifth examining the research on cognitive changes that take place in later adulthood. The last chapter explores psychosocial processes such as coping, adaptation, retirement, and death in old age.

LIFE-CYCLE THEORIES

A variety of theories have delineated either stages or tasks of development that take place at various ages. The more comprehensive theories describe a series of steps that take place throughout the life cycle; the others tend to focus on delineating processes within a specific age period. Theories focusing on the complete life cycle present general outlines of the process of development but explain neither why the proposed patterns occur nor what the nature of the interaction of the biological, social, and psychological spheres is. They do, however, provide a framework for understanding the human life cycle as a sequential progression. We will review several of these life-span theories, but our focus will be on development in the adult years.

Havighurst

Havighurst (1972) proposed a series of life stages, each represented by unique developmental tasks. The tasks arise at certain periods of the individual's life, and successful completion leads to happiness at that period; later success is dependent on the completion of earlier tasks. Havighurst divided the life span into six periods, three of which pertain to adulthood: early adulthood, between 18 and 35; middle adulthood, between 35 and 60; and later maturity, beyond that age. The specific developmental tasks for each age include:

Early Adulthood — selecting a mate
learning to live with a marriage partner
starting a family
rearing children
managing a home
beginning an occupation
assuming civic responsibility
finding social groups

Middle Adulthood — achieving adult civic and social responsibility
establishing and maintaining an economic
standard of living

helping teenage children to become responsible,
  happy adults
developing adult leisure activities
relating to the spouse as a person
accepting and adapting to physiological changes
adjusting to aging parents

Later Maturity—   adjusting to declining physical strength and
  health
adjusting to retirement and reduced income
adjusting to the death of a spouse
establishing relationships within one's age group
meeting social and civic responsibilities
establishing satisfactory physical living
  arrangements

Jung

Although many psychoanalytic theorists emphasize development during childhood, Jung (1960) stressed and identified stages of adult development as well. Jung's first developmental stage actually begins after puberty and extends through ages 35 to 40. He labeled this phase "youth" and saw it as marked by individual development, investment in the outer world, and producing and caring for children. During this period the individual must confront giving up the dreams of childhood while generally broadening horizons and actively engaging the world in a concrete, task- and achievement-oriented manner. Sometime between 35 and 40 the next stage is reached, which includes the second half of life. Jung saw this stage as developing slowly through the unconscious rather than in any direct, dramatic way. During this period there is a shift toward contraction, which is characterized by a reduction of outer-directed behavior and an increase in introversion and self-reflection. Throughout the life cycle, but markedly in this phase, the individual attempts to balance opposing life forces (e.g., feminine and masculine traits and behaviors), ultimately reaching for the primary goal of life, "self-actualization." Self-actualization cannot be reached through the outer-directed energy of youth but must be developed through the accumulation of experience tempered with self-reflection. As a person lives the second half of life, a new purpose must unfold for that life to continue to have meaning. Jung saw continued striving for the goals of youth as counterproductive to the development of future-oriented goals. He believed that it is psychologically positive to accept death as a personally meaningful event and to find within it a goal to strive toward that allows for its acceptance. Thus, Jung saw the nature of man's striving, the development of goals, and the direction of energy as changing throughout the life cycle and ultimately leading to self-actualization, marked by a balancing of life's polarities.

Buhler

Charlotte Buhler (1968) was probably the earliest theorist to systematically examine the complete life cycle. Her method involved collecting biographies, letters, diaries, and later, clinical interviews from about 400 people of varying social classes, occupations, and national origins. This information was classified into three categories: (1) activities, such as profession, friends, etc.; (2) subjective responses to activities and events; and (3) accomplishments during the life cycle. Analysis of this information resulted in the identification of five psychosocial stages:

1. birth to 15 – goals are not self-determined
2. 15 to 25 – experimental selection of goals with associated preparation
3. 25 to 45 – definite and specific self-determination of goals
4. 45 to 65 – assessment of the results of striving for goals
5. 65 on – acknowledgment of degree of fulfillment with recognition of success or failure

These psychosocial stages were also compared to five biological phases: (1) progressive growth, continuing to age 15; (2) continued growth (15 to 25), including the ability to reproduce sexually; (3) stability of growth, between 25 and 45; (4) loss of sexual reproductive ability, between 45 and 65; and (5) biological decline, from 65 on.

"In general, Buhler's theory reflects the ongoing parallel between the biological process of growth, stability and decline and the psychosocial process of expansion, culmination and contraction in activities and accomplishments" (Kimmel 1980, p. 10). On the whole this parallel is maintained, but there is a great deal of room for the two curves to diverge, allowing for a good many individual differences. For example, it is quite possible to experience psychosocial productivity during the phase of biological decline. Buhler viewed life as primarily goal-directed, with the formulation of goals being the central unifying principle in the individual's life. According to her theory, goals are gradually set during the first 20 years of life, culminating in a sense of self-fulfillment in later years. Although some individuals may set new goals during the later life phases, people generally begin focusing on retirement and stability at that time.

Kuhlen (1964) has expanded Buhler's theory, especially in the area of the process of growth, culmination, and contraction. He proposed that the growth expansion motives (e.g., achievement, creativity, power) dominate behavior in the first half of life and that as the individual ages, there is a shift to achieving gratification through less active, more indirect ways. From this perspective the life cycle is marked by the two basic tendencies of growth-expansion and contraction. At some point in midlife, there would seem to be a shift between the two. For Buhler it occurs in the period of self-assessment (ages 45 to 50); for Kuhlen the time of transition is not clearly defined and may be related to a variety of social/psychological/physical events.

Erikson

Erik Erikson (1963, 1968, 1976) divided the life cycle into eight ages or phases. The first four relate to childhood, the fifth to adolescence, and the last three to adulthood. Erikson outlined a series of psychosocial crises crucial to an individual's development. These crises present the potential for continued growth or maladjustment, depending on how they are resolved. As each crisis is faced, a specific psychosocial strength is developed that contributes to further development. Erikson saw each phase as marked by a predominant crisis, and believed that sequential resolution is crucial, but he stated clearly that resolution of one stage does not invariably lead to resolution of the next and that elements of each crisis are present in some form throughout each of the phases.

As the phases of childhood and adolescence have been described in the first developmental volume in this series (Billingham 1981), only the stages that occur during the adult life cycle will be reviewed. Each crisis is marked by a pair of opposite qualities that must be integrated and resolved in order to result in necessary ego development. The resolution ends in the development of a particular human strength, such as hope, will, purpose, competence, fidelity, love, care, or wisdom. Erikson's sixth stage, young adulthood (ages 20 to 40), involves the struggle between intimacy and isolation, with the capacity for love as the desired resolution. True intimacy cannot be achieved until the earlier identity crisis of adolescence is re-solved. In the stage of young adulthood, the individual either develops the capacity to make commitments to the self and others or avoids intimacy, which leads to isolation rather than love based on mutual devotion. Mid-dle adulthood (ages 40 to 65) is marked by the struggle between "gen-erativity" and "stagnation," with the resolution leading to "care." The individual must also deal with the issues of productivity and creativity as they relate to the opposites of the self and others. These polarities incorporate pride and pleasure, an enriched life, and guidance for later generations on the one side and an egocentric, nonproductive life approach marked by self-indulgence and personal impoverishment on the other. This stage is the longest and is primarily concerned with the production of something that will outlive the self. The last stage, that of old age or maturity, is marked by the struggle between "integrity" and "despair" stimulated by the growing awareness of death and involving the evaluation of one's life and accomplishments. A sense of integrity develops from the understanding, appreciation, and acceptance of one's life as having had meaning; despair stems from the sense of one's life having been meaningless or wasted. Integrity allows the acceptance of death, the final stage of life; despair leads to fear of death and a loss of faith in the self and others.

While these stages take up a good many years of one's life and the crises are fairly general, Peck (1968) has attempted to define more precisely the issues of these ages. He proposed seven critical tasks, of which four are in the middle years and three in the later years:

1. Valuing wisdom rather than physical power.
2. Socialization rather than sexualization of human relationships, allowing greater depth of understanding and enhancing the marital relationship when children are leaving home.
3. Cathectic flexibility versus cathectic impoverishment, leading to emotional openness with a wider range of relationships that replace ties broken when children leave home and friends die.
4. Mental flexibility versus mental rigidity.
5. Ego differentiation versus work-role preoccupation, allowing for the development of a wider range of meaningful activities to replace the loss of a work role.
6. Body transcendence versus body preoccupation, allowing the enjoyment of life despite the inevitable physical decline or deterioration.
7. Ego transcendence versus ego preoccupation, resulting in finding meaning in life through more than one's current activities or actions.

RESEARCH ON STAGES OF ADULTHOOD

Recently a number of researchers have begun to explore the events that occur and the issues that are dealt with throughout the period of adulthood. The goal of these studies (which will be reviewed briefly below) has been to identify the sequence of psychosocial development between the ages of approximately 20 and 60. This research has resulted in a variety of perspectives on adult development that have not as yet been integrated.

Questions raised concern the nature of development at these times and the relationship between change and time. It is possible that change through the adult life cycle takes place in several ways. It can be explained on the basis of individual events that occur idiosyncratically and trigger change and growth whenever they occur. It is possible, instead, that people progress through specific life stages in a fairly consistent, specific order that is standard or universal in some way. Finally, development may be linked to chronological age and may proceed in an invariable sequence. These perspectives highlight one of the central questions of development in adulthood. Does development proceed through an orderly, predictable sequence based on some kind of internal triggering mechanism, or is development contingent on external events and their impact on the individual? There is currently no direct answer to this question, but it is likely that Neugarten's (1979) view and Kimmel's (1980) conclusions may best represent the current state of knowledge. Adult development, in all likelihood, involves an interaction between internally triggered and controlled experiences and external events that appears to be linked in some way to age and social expectations; however, it can be greatly altered by external events and individual idiosyncrasies.

A study by Levinson (1978) involved a small sample (40 subjects) of men between the ages of 35 and 45. All were from the same geographical area, but the sample included both blue- and white-collar workers with some minor variation in ethnic background. The study itself was cross-sectional in design and included for each subject a total of 10–20 hours of taped interviews over a 2–3 month period as well as a 2-year follow-up interview. The data gathered included biographical material of the complete life span. The purpose of the study was to identify "relatively universal, genotypic, age linked adult developmental periods" (Levinson et al. 1977, p. 49). The researchers were surprised to find little variability in the age at which each period began. In their view, specific transitions are closely linked to chronological age, and the sequence was found to be consistent across individuals. For Levinson, early adulthood begins after a transition period from adolescence that occurs between the ages of 17 and 22. During this period the individual separates from his or her parents and begins functioning more independently. Following this are the periods of entering the adult world, the transition at age 30, and the settling-down period just prior to age 40. From the ages of 40 to 45 occurs the period of midlife transition that leads the entry into middle adulthood (age 40 to 60). Middle adulthood includes an entry period, a transition at age 50, and finally a culmination period leading to a late-adulthood transition period. In Levinson's scheme, periods of stability alternate with more stressful periods during which change occurs.

The Grant study, published by Vaillant (1977), is the only longitudinal study in this area. It was conducted with 94 male graduates of several elite northeastern colleges. The subjects were selected from a larger sample that had been studied earlier; at the time of this follow-up the average age of the subjects was 47. A variety of psychological, physical, physiological, and cognitive data was collected through a series of questionnaires and interviews. Information on childhood development was collected from families, and the participants were sent yearly follow-up questionnaires after graduating from college. Between 1950 and 1952 each subject was interviewed at home, and in 1969 Vaillant conducted an extensive follow-up interview with those in his sample. Vaillant had intended to be able to predict future success (in job, family, and so on) from the original data gathered during the college years; however, he was surprised at the degree of variability in outcome. He concluded that the life cycle for adults appears to be "more than an invariant sequence of stages with single predictable outcomes." He saw the early adulthood years (adolescence to age 40) concerned primarily with intimacy and career development. He did not find a distinct period of settling-down, as Levinson did. He did identify a period of midlife crisis at about age 40 but did not feel that it is generally a period of upheaval and drama. It is followed by a midlife period that is essentially concerned with issues of generativity, as in Erikson's framework.

Gould (1972, 1978) reported on a series of studies of two samples: 125 males and females who were participating in outpatient psychotherapy groups set up on the basis of age (16–18, 18–22, 22–28, 29–34, 35–43, 43–50, and 50 and above); and 524 middle-class individuals, ranging in age from 16 to 60, who were not in psychotherapy but were selected through personal contacts. The groups were observed and rated on the basis of their characteristics, and differences between the age groups were examined. The larger individual sample was evaluated with a questionnaire administered once, consisting of questions developed from the observed age characteristics delineated in the group study. Gould saw adult development as an ongoing struggle against the constraints of childhood ideas and illusions. At each age a set of characteristic issues, composed of a series of assumptions that must be let go of, are worked on. These assumptions are based on childhood views of the world that are tied to issues of fair play, parental protection, ultimate dependence, self-acceptance, safety, reward, and others. Although the task of revealing and accepting these assumptions as illusory tends to occur at predictable times, Gould also acknowledged fluctuations in these patterns that are tied to individual differences in personality, life-style, and subculture.

Two other major books have dealt with the developmental process through adulthood. Sheehy (1976), in her book *Passages,* drew on much of the literature in this area and on interview data that she gathered independently to identify the sequence of the adult life cycle. Although this book was built around personal observations and reflections more than on research data, it served to popularize this area and stimulate interest in more rigorous research. A second book, by Lowenthal, Thurnher, Chiriboga, and Associates (1975), explored specific points of transition in people's lives rather than the entire adult life span. Four groups were studied (high school seniors, newlyweds, middle-aged parents, and pre-retirement couples). Each group was nearing a major transition period and an attempt was made to examine the process of change and adaptation and its impact on the subjects' lives. The emphasis in the next two chapters will be on the work of Levinson, Gould, and Vaillant, but these other studies will also be referred to, as they add to our understanding of young and middle adulthood. The majority of these studies have fairly severe limitations in terms of generalizability. On the whole, they include primarily white, middle-class adults from approximately the same historical period and do not include an equal number of women. The Vaillant and Levinson studies were conducted with only men as the research population; thus, only some inferences about women can be drawn from them. This research should be considered only a beginning; much broader population samples need to be looked at before any general conclusions can be drawn. Issues of methodology will be examined briefly in the following section.

METHODOLOGY

The purpose of developmental psychology is to understand the growth sequence that individuals experience in the biological, psychological, and social spheres as well as the interaction between these areas. Age is used as the marker for developmental events, and any research methodology must result in an understanding of the sequence of developmental events and of the acquisition and deterioration of abilities; above all, it must be able to distinguish these events and classify them into age-related sequences. Typically, two types of studies are used in this research — longitudinal and cross-sectional. Each has benefits and deficits, and they also share certain difficulties.

Conceptually, the longitudinal study would make the most sense for studying changes over time. In this type of design a group of subjects is evaluated (e.g., in terms of personality and intelligence) at some point in time. The subjects are then followed for an extended period, perhaps throughout the life course, and consistently evaluated at regular intervals to assess changes that may take place in the variables being examined. The results of the successive evaluations are then compared, and any differences would be identified as age changes.

There are a number of difficulties with this type of study. Because of their long-term nature, longitudinal studies are very expensive projects. The length of the project often makes it difficult to maintain the initial sample. Subjects may drop out or die before the study is completed, and very often the reasons for dropout are related to the variables being studied. For example, if intelligence is being looked at, it may be that those who remain in the study are more intelligent than the dropouts; then the overall intelligence levels achieved for the group in later years would be higher. Finally, in this type of study the measures taken must be consistent over the course of the study, or at least comparable tests must be designed so that the same variable is being measured at each stage. It is often difficult to meet these requirements, and if the same tests are being used, they are likely to be more relevant at one age than at another. This is generally true of longitudinal studies as a whole; e.g., a project that was designed to explore a variety of age-related variables in the 1940s would not be responsive to social, methodological, or technical changes since then that may make the original questions and design somewhat outdated or less valuable at later points.

In cross-sectional studies, a group of subjects of a variety of ages is selected at one point. For a study of the utilization of medical services across the life span, for example, subjects may progress in age from their 20s to their 70s at 10-year intervals. One would then have six groups of subjects who will all be questioned at a particular time to study this variable. One of the major problems of this type of study is due to *cohort effects.* A cohort is a group of people who are born at about the same time and thus live through and are influenced by the same social, cultural, and historical factors at about the same time in their lives. Therefore, each age group in a study may have been differentially affected by events throughout their lives, which may in turn affect the variables being studied. In general, the cross-sectional design is useful for describing differences among groups born during different eras, but it does not provide clear information about changes that occur specifically due to the aging process. The results of this research method, therefore, tend to confound age and cohort.

Schaie (1977) reported on a different research approach that uses *sequential* designs in order to solve some of these methodological problems. These appear to have the potential to help discriminate the confounded effects of age, cohort, and time of measurement that are inherent in both cross-sectional and longitudinal designs. There are three types of sequential designs: cross-sequential, time-sequential, and cohort-sequential. The cross-sequential design involves combining elements of the cross-sectional and longitudinal designs; it is probably the most practical of the three sequential designs. Because the other sequential designs have not been used as much and are more impractical and time-consuming, we will describe only the cross-sequential design. This method involves selecting several cohorts that are followed over a period of time. For instance, intelligence may be studied by selecting six groups of subjects between 20 and 70 years of age (one group for each ten-year age spread). These subjects would be evaluated at a particular time, as in a cross-sectional study, but would also be followed and retested at a later time. This would combine longitudinal elements with the cross-sectional design and allow the separation of cohort and time-of-measurement effects. These designs have not been much used yet; however, they may become more important in the future (Botwinick 1978).

PHYSIOLOGICAL AND PSYCHOLOGICAL DEVELOPMENT IN YOUNG AND MIDDLE ADULTHOOD

Physiological Development

In general, there are no biologically based phases of adult life because there are few physiological changes (of which menopause is one) that occur in any orderly age progression. Changes during the early and middle years are gradual and tend to affect a variety of organ systems and abilities. In normal development, the results of these changes begin to be seen during late-middle adulthood (around age 60). The changes vary from system to system, with some beginning earlier in this cycle and others delayed until later in life. Coupled with this variation between organ systems is a great deal of variation due to individual differences tied to genetic factors, nutrition, living environment, exercise, and the like. In the following discussion, all age markers should be considered approximate averages, with a wide degree of possible variation around these central points.

Young adulthood is the period of peak physiological development, and most bodily functions are fully developed by the mid-twenties. Skeletal growth is completed by around 25 years of age (Tanner 1978); however, some minor growth can still be achieved because of continued growth of the vertebral column until age 30. The muscular system seems to show parallel development; peak strength and efficiency are typically reached in the mid-20s to early 30s (Timiras 1972). Age does not seem to have as much effect on the functioning of the smooth muscles as it does on the striped musculature. In the striped muscles there is a loss of about 10% in muscle strength between the ages of 30 and 60, but there are wide individual differences. The degree of loss is directly proportional to the level of activity and exercise. Appropriate exercise can maintain strength throughout early and middle adulthood; strength can continue to increase during this period as well. It is generally agreed that the primary areas of muscle decline are in the back and legs and that postural changes with age are not a function of age itself but are related to postural habits and disease processes (Bischoff 1976).

Changes in external features, although not generally evident in early adulthood, do begin at this time. After adolescence, the skin gradually loses moisture, and lines and wrinkles begin to appear. Changes in hair, both graying and balding, begin at this time as well. These changes are generally tied to heredity and degree of scalp blood circulation, but most people take them as signs of aging and deterioration. Throughout the life cycle, there are continual changes in the functioning of the senses. Again, visual acuity is best at about age 20 and remains relatively constant until around age 40. At that time there is a slow decline. Other changes related to structural properties of the eyes appear to take place at an earlier age. As the eye ages, the lens becomes more opaque and less elastic, which produces changes in shape leading to deterioration in accommodation and convergence. Typically, middle-aged people require corrective glasses for reading, and because the pupil's size decreases more light is needed for effective vision. Therefore, recovery from glare and adaptation to the dark take longer in middle age. Generally, peripheral vision gradually shrinks during the middle years and at about age 55 reaches stability again.

A variety of studies (Bischoff 1976) have demonstrated a gradual decline in hearing with age. Although the techniques for this research are well documented, other factors, such as age-related cautiousness, attitudinal changes, and motivation, affect these results. On the whole, however, a decrease in the ability to discriminate pitch begins around the age of 25, and at about age 55 there is a more marked drop. After age 55 there is a continual decline in hearing, especially at the upper sound frequencies. Although this hearing loss occurs for both sexes, it is generally accepted that women hear better than men at all age levels past 50 to 60. Sensitivity to both taste and smell appear to be fairly consistent; there is little change in these functions up until the ages of 50 to 60. With aging there is a decrease in the number of taste buds in each papilla, and this change occurs somewhat earlier for women than for men (40 to 45 versus 50 to 60). Finally, sensitivity to touch tends to increase up to age 45 and then decreases quite markedly. Sensitivity to pain remains fairly steady until age 50 and then changes differentially for different parts of the body. Pain tolerance may decrease; however, pain appears to be a sensation that is highly affected by culture, ethnic group, affect, motivation, and so on (Bischoff 1976; Troll 1975; Rogers 1979).

The cardiovascular system reaches adult size and rhythm by about 16 years of age, and the function, rate, and rhythm of the heart are maintained throughout adulthood with ongoing work and exercise. There appear to be increases with age in serum cholesterol levels and a steady, slow rise in blood pressure (Draheim and Ashburn 1980). In middle age some individuals experience hypertrophy of the left ventricle, which can be related to arteriosclerosis or atherosclerosis. Generally, the respiratory system maintains full efficiency throughout early middle age, and changes involving thickening, stiffening, and reduction in elasticity of lung tissues do not occur until about 55 or 60 years of age. These two systems are interrelated, and both are responsive to environmental factors for maintenance. Weight, diet, exercise, smoking, alcohol consumption, and physical stress, among other factors, can have a profound effect on the maintenance of these systems and subsequent vulnerability to disease. Finally, the gastrointestinal system functions consistently from early adulthood through later periods. There is some decline in gastric secretions as well as in free acid content, total daily acid production, and pepsin content in the stomach. At about age 60, there is a sharp decline in ptyalin (a starch-digesting enzyme in saliva) and in pancreatic digestive enzymes that may be related to the rising incidence of intestinal disorders in later life (Mourad 1980).

As in the other systems mentioned, brain weight reaches a maximum in the mid-20s and declines with age. Along with this goes a gradual reduction in number of nerve cells and actual brain size. The amount of water in the brain is lowest in the mid-20s and remains fairly constant until the 70s. What may be more important than actual brain size is the maintenance of functions and abilities, and it is this brain efficiency that is closely affected by both blood flow and pulmonary intake of oxygen. There is a gradual reduction in these functions with age, and the development of vascular changes affects them greatly. Sleep is another area of physiological functioning that shows consistent changes with aging. During middle and late adulthood total sleep time tends to decrease. The proportion of time spent in REM (rapid eye movement) versus nonREM sleep appears to remain constant, while the amount of time spent in deeper sleep (stages 3 and 4) tends to be less in older groups.

Sensory and Motor Changes

Reaction time changes directly with age, and this effect holds up fairly well across a variety of studies (Eichorn 1978). Response time is fastest in the late teens and early 20s; it then decreases with age. Within this general framework there is still a great deal of individual variation, as well as variation related to particular tasks. Performance on simple reaction-time or manual tasks tends to hold up well into the 60s and then declines, while slowing may appear much earlier on more complex tasks, such as tracking a moving target. On most tasks, although reaction time changes and the amount of overall output declines with age, it appears that level of accuracy is not appreciably affected. It is still not clear what accounts for these findings. It is possible that a variety of factors, such as central nervous system changes, motivational factors, or practice, may all be involved in the process.

Intelligence and Memory

The traditional view of changes in memory and intelligence is that these abilities peak in the late teens and early 20s and gradually decline from that point on (Troll 1975). However, more recent evidence indicates that this is not necessarily the case. These functions are no longer considered unidemensional; rather, they are complex functions with multiple components. Currently distinctions are made between different aspects of intelligence ("fluid" versus "crystallized") and several memory components (sensory, primary, and secondary). There appear to be different rates and degree of decline in each of the aspects; however, decline does not seem to take place until the late 50s and 60s. Furthermore, performance is often related to a variety of other variables, such as motivation, reaction time, and perceptual integrative functions. The design of these studies affects the interpretations and conclusions drawn; the results are often conflicting. All these factors will be fully reviewed in Chapter 6.

Personality

Personality is a complex phenomenon that includes not only acts of behavior but also feelings, attitudes, values, and interpersonal relationships. Early theorists saw personality developing through childhood and adolescence, resulting in a set of traits or characteristics that remain constant throughout adulthood. The development of life-span psychology has recently begun to explore aspects of change and stability throughout the complete life cycle. The questions being asked fall into two general categories: (1) Do personality variables remain constant over time, or do they change with age for the individual? and (2) are there age-consistent patterns of change in personality that cut across individuals so that some variables are more consistently seen at one age than another? In this area as in others, a number of methodological difficulties make general conclusions difficult. These consist of differences between cross-sectional and longitudinal studies; the lack of control for intellectual and socioeconomic status; the invalidity or unreliability of some of the instruments used to measure a particular personality variable; questions about whether the concepts studied mean the same thing to each age group that is measured (e.g., does aggression represent the same set of behaviors and feelings to a 20-year-old as to a 60-year-old); and the failure of most studies to account for the effects of intervening variables (e.g., marriage, children, illness) on personality factors. Despite these limitations, a great many studies do shed some light on changes in personality over the life span.

Neugarten (1977) reviewed a number of cross-sectional studies of a variety of personality features and their association with age, such as egocentrism, dependency, introversion, dogmatism, cautiousness, conformity, risk taking, locus of control, and happiness. She concluded that the findings are extremely inconsistent—for each variable some investigators found age-consistent changes, but others did not. The only apparent exception is introversion, which tends to increase with age in the second half of life. In a better-controlled cross-sequential study, Schaie and Parham (1976) examined nineteen personality traits in a group of 21- to 84-year-olds over a 7-year period. Their conclusions were that seventeen of these traits were stable over time and that changes appeared to be related more to cohort differences than age differences. In a series of multidimensional studies conducted through the University of Chicago (Neugarten and Associates 1964), a large group of 40- through 80-year-olds was studied utilizing a variety of objective and projective tests and intensive interviews. These studies do show some consistent findings. There seems to be a general change from active mastery of the environment to a more passive, less involved relationship to life events. There is also a consistent trend toward interiority. This study, which tends to confirm the theories of Jung and others, also found sex differences in personality development. It appears that older men become more aware of and receptive to affiliative, nurturant, and sensual feelings, while women tend to become more in touch with their aggressive and egocentric impulses. These findings were also supported in a study by Thurnher (1971). These studies did not discover any age-related differences in other personality dimensions, such as goal-directed behaviors, coping styles, or satisfaction with life.

As the cross-sectional studies reported above tend to reflect differences that occur at various ages rather than age changes, longitudinal studies need to be examined. Few of these studies are currently available; however, in an early study by Kelly (1955) both men and women were tested in their 20s and again in their 40s. The study found that consistency over this period was highest for values (aesthetic, religious, economic, social, political, and theoretical) and occupational interests but low for self-ratings and other personality variables. Other studies (Woodruff and Birren 1972; D. H. Heath, cited in Birren and Schaie 1977) seem to indicate that constancy is more typical than change. Another multidimensional longitudinal study conducted at the Institute of Human Development in Berkeley has identified a variety of personality types and traced the changes in their patterns over several age periods (Block 1971; Peskin 1972; Haan and Day, 1974). Although they did find that certain general changes took place and that there were sex differences, they concluded that on the whole each personality type remained stable and recognizable over time.

In view of the lack of consistency and methodological problems in this research area it is difficult to draw any direct conclusions from these data. However, they give the general impression that personality is relatively stable over the life span and that individual differences may be more important than age-related changes. Perhaps the clearest age-related change consists of the growth of interiority, or the redirection of energy and attention from the outside to the internal world. This theory was first formulated by Cumming and Henry (1961); termed "disengagement theory," it holds that some time after the 40s adults begin to withdraw from the social and physical world. This theory as well as other aspects of personality change will be dealt with more completely in Chapters 4, 5, and 6. According to the theory, this process begins in the middle years and continues through old age rather than occurring spontaneously with advanced age. We should also note that this concept is fairly controversial; researchers have proposed that it be replaced by the concept of "attachment" (Knudtson 1976; Kalish and Knudtson 1976), which is conceived of more broadly. This concept takes into account natural changes that occur in attachment through the life cycle, which may be brought about by deaths, divorce, loss of children, and other processes.

Sexuality

Sexuality is one of the most central aspects of human behavior that is both affected by and affects psychological, physiological, social, and cultural aspects of life. In recent years, following the early publication of the work of Masters and Johnson (1966), a great deal of research about this area of human functioning has been done. A complete discussion of all aspects of sexuality is beyond the scope of this monograph, but this section will present information on the human sexual response and changes that take place with age for both males and females.

Masters and Johnson (1966) delineated four distinct phases of physiological sexual responses: (1) the excitement phase, (2) the plateau phase, (3) orgasm, and (4) resolution. During the excitement stage psychological and/or physiological stimulation leads to arousal that is characterized by an erection in the male and, in the female, vaginal lubrication, an increase in the diameter of the clitoris, and increased blood congestion in the labia minor and major. This phase typically occurs more quickly in men than in women; however, once effective stimulation is produced, erection and vaginal lubrication occur within 10 seconds. This phase can last from several minutes to several hours; however, as stimulation continues, the next phase, plateau, is reached. Physiologically, this phase is marked in the male by an increase in the size and an elevation of the testes. In women, there is constriction of the vaginal barrel (termed the orgasmic platform), breast size increases up to 25%, and the clitoris elevates and contracts. For both sexes this phase is marked by a high degree of blood congestion and sexual tension in the entire pelvic area that results in a variety of color changes in the genital area as well as in other parts of the body. This phase can last from 30 seconds to several minutes.

The third stage, that of orgasm, consists of two parts for men. Initially there are slight contractions of the genital organs, resulting in a subjective sense of ejaculatory inevitability. This is then followed by the ejaculation itself, which is produced by the same contracted muscles and consists of two to three expulsive efforts occurring quite quickly followed by a slowing of contractions and expulsion. These rhythmic spasms involve the prostate, seminal vesicles, vas deferens, and urethra, and the contractions occur at intervals of 8/10 of a second. The female orgasm is characterized by a longer period of contractions (from three to twelve) of the vaginal orgasmic platform. Concurrent with this are sequential smooth-muscle contractions of the uterus, flowing downward to the cervix. Although the speed at which women reach orgasm is affected by the nature of stimulation (vaginal versus clitoral), there is no physiological difference between the orgasms that occur with either type. Both sexes experience contractions of other skeletal muscles and the rectal sphincter muscle as well as increases in blood pressure (10–40 mm rise in both systolic and diastolic) and heart rate (rises to 120–160 beats per minute). The orgasmic phase lasts from 3 to 15 seconds and can be considered a "psychophysiological experience" in that it involves the integration of subjective perceptions and a peak physical reaction to sexual stimuli, followed by a period of physical release from vasoconstriction. The last stage, resolution, involves the disgorgement of blood from the genitalia and the body's return to its resting state. When orgasm occurs, resolution is fairly rapid (although in women it proceeds more slowly than in men); however, if orgasm does not occur, the process is much lengthier (from 2 to 6 hours) and is associated with irritability and pain in the genital area.

As described above, there are many similarities between the male and female sexual cycles; however, there are marked differences between the two as well (Kolodny, Masters, and Johnson 1979). Perhaps the most distinct difference is in the period following orgasm. Men have a refractory period, which can last from several minutes to several hours, during which they cannot achieve further orgasm. The length of this period, besides depending on individual differences, changes with age, so that younger men are capable (at one extreme) of having several orgasms within a 10-minute period, while those over 30 tend to take longer and require complete resolution and a new response cycle. In contrast to this, women are physiologically capable of experiencing multiple orgasms within a brief period without a loss of sexual tension below the plateau level. Masters and Johnson (1966) also identified three patterns of female sexual response: type A, a pattern of multiple orgasms with a return to the plateau phase between each; type B, which does not result in a complete orgasm but remains at the plateau level, creating sexual frustrations; and type C, which is considered a maximal orgasm lasting longer than the other types, followed by a refractory period as in the male. This last type can also be preceded by a series of type A orgasms. Other differences between men and women involve the following: (1) Males can maintain the orgasmic response despite distractions or the cessation of stimulation; for women, if stimulation is stopped so is orgasm; and (2) the excitement phase lasts longer in women.

As people age, there are changes in their sexual functioning as well as physiological changes (Kolodny, Masters, and Johnson 1979; Wolman and Money 1980). However, a majority of the literature indicates that most of the changes in functioning are related more to psychological changes than to actual physical changes. Perhaps the best predictor of later sexual behavior is the individual's sexual behavior throughout the life cycle. Generally, males experience orgasm from puberty on but peak sometime around the age of 20. In contrast, orgasm for women becomes more frequent and peaks during the adult years between 26 and 40. This difference in sexual cycle can have important implications for relationships and must be considered in adult sexuality. Other changes in women as they age are drops in circulating levels of estrogen and progesterone, which are stable until menopause is reached and then steadily decline; structural changes in the ovaries; and morphological changes in the reproductive tract and external genitalia (e.g., a 50% drop in uterine weight, thinning and shrinking of the vaginal wall, slower vaginal lubrication). However, with these physiological changes there is no change in the woman's capacity to reach orgasm.

It appears that males experience a wider variety of changes with age than women do and that these can affect sexual functioning, generally through their effect on the males' psychological state. Up to the age of 40 androgen levels remain fairly constant; they then begin to decline so that at age 65 they are 30% lower and at age 75 they are 85–90% lower. There are ongoing changes in testicular tissue and a steady drop in the production of sperm, although these changes vary enormously across individuals. It should also be noted that although there are consistent reductions in sperm with age, there is little change or reduction in seminal fluid. There are also structural changes in the prostate gland with age but, again, this involves a great deal of variability. Prostate changes can have an important effect on sexual functioning, as can surgery for prostate conditions in later life. More specifically, there are concrete changes in the male's sexual ability as he ages. There is a reduced amount of ejaculate and the force of ejaculation diminishes. Generally, the time to achieve erection is longer with age, and the refractory period increases as well (for adolescents it is only a few minutes; for men aged 30, half an hour or less; and for men aged 50, as much as 8 to 24 hours). As males age, statistically there appears to be an increase in impotence (for men in their 50s, 8%; in their 70s, 27%; and at age 75, 55%). As males become older, they can also maintain their erections longer, it may take them longer to reach orgasm, and they may lose their erections immediately following orgasm.

Overall, there appears to be a reduction of frequency of sexual interactions with age that is not necessarily tied to changes in physiological functioning. These changes seem more directly related to changes in attitudes, psychological factors, and changes in interests and priorities. Despite this drop in activity, survey data indicate that at age 60, 94% of males and 84% of females are still sexually active (frequency of sexual intercourse was not considered). There is a drop in frequency as people age; a 1972 survey indicated a frequency of 3.25/week for 18–24-year-olds, 2/week for 35–45-year-olds, 1/week for those over 45. All these figures are higher than for another sample taken in 1942 (Wolman and Money 1980). Changes in sampling and in people's inhibitions may have played a part in this difference, but it appears that generally people are more active sexually in this era than earlier ones, even though a drop in activity still takes place with age. A longitudinal study at Duke University (Wolman and Money 1980) indicated that for adults aged 60–94 there is a lower level of sexual functioning for women than for men and that women report less interest in sex than men do. As this cannot be accounted for by physiological changes, other factors must be responsible. An important cause may be the limited availability of partners for women in later life, since death typically occurs earlier for males, and women make up a larger percentage of the elderly population. We may conclude that there is a decline in sexual activity as one ages and that it is greater for women than men, regardless of the age period studied.

Menopause and Climacteric

Between the ages of approximately 48 and 51, women experience a change in hormonal patterns. There is evidence that the ovaries no longer respond to pituitary follicle-stimulating hormone (FSH) and that there is a decrease in estrogen production. During this time ovulation ceases, leading to an ending of reproductive capabilities (climacteric). There is some variation in the age when this occurs, and many women experience an irregular cycle for a time prior to the termination of the menses. Historically, it has been thought that menopausal women experience a variety of physiological and psychological symptoms. Some have considered that these indicate that the loss of reproductive ability represents a major crisis for women. Symptoms associated with menopause include hot flashes, flushing, excessive sweating, dyspareunia, insomnia, irritability, nervousness, depression, fatigue, palpitations, and headaches, among others. More recently, it has been found that only a few of these symptoms can be directly related to hormonal changes and that the others are associated with psychological factors (Ballinger 1981). Hot flashes, dyspareunia, excessive sweating, and possibly insomnia seem to be tied to decreases in estrogen levels, and they are indeed responsive to estrogen-replacement therapy. At this time, however, estrogen replacement is a fairly controversial procedure because of the possibility of increased risk of cancer (Ballinger 1981).

Psychological symptoms are seen in some women, but more extensive research indicates that these symptoms are not typical in menopausal women. There does not appear to be an increase in these symptoms during this period; earlier work may have been subject to bias because assumptions were made based only on women who were seeing physicians because of problems. When broader populations have been studied, there is typically no increase in emotional disturbance when compared to nonmenopausal women. These problems are often tied to psychological issues other than menopause (Kimmel 1980). Neugarten, Wood, Kraines, and Loomis (1968) have reported that women in middle age are not concerned about impending menopause but fear becoming widows. In fact many women see this time as one of more sexual freedom, as they do not have to be concerned about pregnancy.

There is a clear marker of physiological change in women; this is not the case for men. A developing body of data indicates that men may also experience hormonal cycles and shifts that may have an effect on their moods and performance (Ramey 1972; Parlee 1978). As men age there is a slow decrease in testosterone levels; however, these levels are not necessarily related to fertility. Some middle-aged men do experience a constellation of symptoms that involve mood disturbances (depression, anxiety, irritability, and indecisiveness), sexual inadequacy, and vaguely defined physical complaints. This has been termed the "male climacteric"; at this time its relation to drops in testosterone levels has not been confirmed (Henker 1981). Although declining testosterone levels may play some part, it is more likely that men who experience these symptoms are responding to an interaction between sociocultural aspects of aging and physical slowing down.

TRANSITIONS: COPING AND ADAPTATION

Throughout adulthood, the individual experiences a wide range of events, both internally and externally precipitated, that can lead to changes in environment, attitudes, self-perception, relationships, and behaviors. Many of these events (for example, graduation, marriage, retirement) can be predicted on the basis of typical timing within a particular culture. Others can occur quite randomly and, in fact, do not occur for all people (for example, divorce). Any of these events can lead to a crisis in people's lives or can become the basis for a period of transition from one state to another. A crisis can be best characterized as a severely upsetting situation, often triggered by a dramatic event, typically involving loss, lasting only a short time, and requiring the summoning of resources to deal with an immediate problem. The outcome of a crisis can be either a return to the preexisting situation or a change instigated by the event. Transitions, however, do not necessarily evolve out of a crisis situation, although they often do. When a crisis leads to change, the individual enters a period of transition in which the changes become integrated into all aspects of the person's life (adaptation). In a more general sense, transitions involve any event that necessitates giving up a set of assumptions about the world or the self and the development of a new set of assumptions to cope with the event. A transition provides the opportunity for psychological growth, but there is also the danger of psychological deterioration. Often both elements are present (Schlossberg 1981). Transitions can be categorized by time periods (passage from one chronological stage in the life cycle to another), by role shifts (changing social roles that require adaptation), and by marker events (events that serve as transformation points).

Specific periods of transition and the events that mark these changes will be described in later chapters. At this time, it is important to gain some broad understanding of the factors associated with the individual's ability to cope with and adapt to the changes that occur throughout adulthood. Adaptation is often dependent on a variety of interacting variables that seem to fall into three categories: (1) characteristics of the transition itself; (2) characteristics of the pretransition and posttransition environments; and (3) characteristics of the individual. The following discussion is based on the work of Schlossberg (1981), who has reviewed and summarized these diverse elements and their impact on adaptation.

The transition itself can be characterized in terms of the nature of the role change—either a role loss or a role gain. This role change interacts with the emotional element of the transition. Transition periods can generate either positive, pleasurable feelings or negative, painful feelings. To a certain extent there is some universality in these feelings, but there are often marked individual differences that may make certain experiences pleasurable for some and negative for others. Events can be triggered by either internal or external factors, and there is a relationship between the nature of the trigger and the sense of control that individuals feel they maintain over their own lives. It is likely that self-generated changes are easier to adapt to than those that are imposed. The timing and onset of the transition is related to adaptation as well. Predictable events can be prepared for, and adaptation to them is easier than for those events that come at unexpected times or at times that may be out of sequence in the typical life cycle. The expected duration of the change – whether it is permanent, temporary, or ambiguous – is another factor that can affect adaptation and coping. Painful changes are easier to tolerate if they are seen as temporary, and if the change is desired, it is adapted to more easily if it is thought to be permanent. The most difficult situation appears to be one in which the change is seen as ambiguous and its duration is not clear. For example, it may be easier to adapt to a terminal illness than to one in which the prognosis is uncertain or the long-term effects are unpredictable. Finally, the level of stress that the transition triggers is a major factor in adaptation. Stress is associated with both positive and negative change. A body of research that looks at the level of stress associated with various life events and the relationship between accumulated stress and the development of illness is reviewed in another volume in this series (Bieliauskas 1981).

The second broad category of factors that affect adaptation is concerned with the characteristics of the pretransition and posttransition environments. The nature and degree of interpersonal support available to the individual has a profound effect on coping; this has been documented through studies of concentration camp survivors and former prisoners of war. There are two important elements of support; both giving and receiving have an effect on adaptation. The desire to help someone else has contributed to survival in a variety of situations. The sense that their presence is valued and needed by others has been shown to have a profound effect on the recovery of burn victims and patients with severe poliomyelitis. Social support can be derived from friends, family, and intimate relationships, and each of these is affected by ethnic background, sex, and socioeconomic status. Intimate relationships involving trust, support, understanding, and the sharing of confidences may be the most important of these variables. (There is some evidence that one factor contributing to earlier death for males may be that it is difficult or even impossible for many males to form intimate ties with others.) Other sources of support include occupational organizations, religious groups, and political, community, and social welfare groups, all of which can be important and may in fact substitute for more primary support systems for some people. The level of support available to a patient undergoing surgery or adjusting to a chronic or life-threatening disease is a crucial factor in recovery and future quality of life. Assessment of support is often necessary, and if little is available the health care staff may themselves fill this role until new systems can be established. Finally, the physical setting in which the transition takes place is important as well. A variety of research has linked the effects of climate, weather, neighborhood factors, living arrangements, workplace, and setting (rural or urban) to level of stress and the ability to cope with transition periods.

The final category involves the characteristics of the individual. It includes such factors as psychosocial competence, sex and sex-role identification, age and life stage at the time of the transition, state of health, race, socioeconomic status, values, and previous experience with similar transitions. We cannot discuss each of these individually, but it may be useful to review several that have primary implications for the developmental aspects of adulthood. Lowenthal, Thurnher, Chiriboga, and Associates (1975) summarized their findings on life stage and coping: The young appear to thrive better with stress than without it; the middle-aged seem to be in a high-risk period when negative stress is more frequent than positive, which often leads to feelings of being overwhelmed; and those in later life generally appear to be better-off psychologically, and better able to cope with change if they have eliminated unwanted duties and obligations. Sex-role identification also seems to be an important factor that shows the intricacy of the interrelationships between individual characteristics, the type of transition, and individual coping ability. For women who have adhered to a stereotyped role (dependence, passivity, and helplessness), adjustment to transitions (e.g., divorce) that demand independence, assertiveness, and self-reliance is often extremely difficult and stressful. For men who may be used to feeling in control, transitions that promote feelings of powerlessness may be very difficult.

It is important to realize that all these factors interact in many ways and that different factors may be more salient for one person than another. As research continues about the nature of transitions and how people adapt to changes in their lives, particular coping styles are being associated with different types of transitions. There is also some evidence that certain styles of coping may be more adaptive at particular life stages. Ability to cope is a complex interaction between the individual, life stage, and social, cultural, and environmental factors; the willingness and ability to understand these issues in the health care setting can be crucial to the delivery of health care services. Illness can be considered a period of transition or, at times, a crisis period, in which all the factors discussed operate to foster or hinder adaptation. A number of researchers have begun to identify variables most crucial to adjustment to illness. An example is the work done by Moos (1979) in identifying the major adaptive tasks necessary in adjusting to illness and the coping processes typically used. The tasks he identified involve

1. dealing with pain and incapacitation
2. dealing with the hospital environment and special treatment procedures

3. developing adequate relationships with professional staff
4. preserving a reasonable emotional balance
5. preserving a satisfactory self-image
6. preserving relationships with family and friends
7. preparing for an uncertain future.

The ability to accomplish these tasks is closely associated with the individual's coping and the eventual outcome of the transition. Moos went on to delineate a number of coping skills or strategies common to those with medical problems: denying or minimizing the seriousness of the problem; dissociating one's emotions from the situation; seeking relevant information and using intellectual resources effectively; requesting reassurance and emotional support from family, friends, and medical staff; learning specific illness-related procedures; setting concrete, limited goals; and rehearsing alternative outcomes, predicting problems that may arise, and trying to prepare for them. Each of these strategies may be used at one time or another during a medical problem; the choice of strategy often relates to the nature of the problem and the personality of the individual involved.

SUMMARY AND CONCLUSIONS

Adulthood does not appear to be marked by predictable physiological or cognitive changes that identify developmental periods. Although young and middle adulthood are characterized by constancy in many physiological and personality variables, they are not stagnant times. Changes do take place, often in response to events that occur during these periods. Havighurst, Jung, Erikson, and Buhler have identified various tasks and stages of adulthood, and more recently, research has begun to delineate these stages and their themes in more detail. A number of sampling problems with these studies, however, prevent broad generalization at this time. It is important to be aware of the research methodology used (cross-sectional, longitudinal, cross-sequential), as different methodologies may require different methods of data interpretation. Finally, adulthood is marked by periods of transition that can be characterized in many ways. These periods can be precipitated by a variety of factors or events, and the individual's ability to cope with and adapt to them, and style of doing so, are extremely important to adult development.

YOUNG ADULTHOOD: AGES 18 THROUGH 40

DEVELOPMENTAL PERIODS

The studies of adult development introduced in Chapter 1 delineate a number of stages of adulthood. Each stage appears to entail particular tasks or issues, and although these are not necessarily exclusive to each period, there is some evidence that particular themes dominate certain stages. Although the limitations of the major studies make it difficult to generalize their findings to populations other than those studied (white, middle-class males predominantly), this research is important; it has laid the groundwork for the examination of the adult life cycle and has begun to identify the many factors and issues active through these periods.

Through his study of men, Levinson (1977, 1978) viewed the evolution of a "life structure" as the central process of adult development. This evolution is ongoing, taking place through a series of alternating periods of stability and transition. The life structure itself consists of three aspects:

1. The nature of a man's *sociocultural world,* including class, religion, ethnicity, race, family, political systems, occupational structure, and particular conditions and events, such as economic depression or prosperity, war, and liberation movements of all kinds.
2. His *participation in this world,* the individual's evolving relationships and roles as citizen, worker, boss, lover, friend, husband, father, and member of diverse groups and organizations.
3. The *aspects of the self* that are expressed and lived out in the various components of his life, and the aspects of the self that must be inhibited or neglected within the life structure (Levinson 1977, p. 100).

For Levinson the life structure involves the patterning of equally important aspects and evolves through tasks at each stage that involve decision making about goals and values. During periods of transition, the individual must deal with the termination of the old life structure and the task of building a new one. This task involves self-examination, exploration of other directions, and movement toward decisions that build a new life structure for the next phase of stability. Each age period, in this schema, is defined by a primary developmental task and not by significant events such as deaths or marriage, which can occur at any age.

The years from 17 to 22 constitute the period of early adult transition that involves leaving the family and entering the adult world while giving up adolescent views and relationships. At this stage individuals begin to separate from their parents, emotionally and often financially, to develop a more independent life structure. It is often a period of great change that can involve feelings of loss, fear, and insecurity. Kimmel (1980) reported that during this period a majority of people in Levinson's study moved away from their parents either geographically or socially and that 20% had serious conflicts with parents that lasted several years. For many, moving away meant settling in other institutional settings, such as college or the army, which served as a halfway point between independence and a semistructured, supportive environment. This is also the period in which, according to Levinson, the Dream is formed; it represents an inner sense of how the individual wants life to work out. It can include realistic ideas and plans as well as fantasies and can be related to work, family, or the community.

This period is followed by a more tranquil time (ages 22 to 28) tied to more active involvement in the adult world. There appear to be two contrasting features or tasks at this stage: exploring life's possibilities while keeping options open and, at the same time, making choices about work and marriage that lead to defining goals and making commitments. There are a variety of approaches to resolving this conflict. One can either keep a loose structure generally, make some strong commitments while holding others, or make most major choices and commitments at this time. At this stage 75% of the sample had made both marital and occupational choices.

During this stage two special relationships tend to develop that can be important for growth, but not necessary—the Mentor and the Special Woman. The Mentor relationship is a strong association with an older, more experienced man (in this sample there were no female mentors; however, Levinson felt that women can serve in this role and also that the relationship is equally important and possible for both men and women) who serves as a support and guide into a particular field and in realizing the Dream. In the initial phase of the relationship the Mentor is typically in a superior position, but the relationship equalizes over time until it comes to an end in a later life stage. The Special Woman, who may or may not be a wife, also helps in the realization of the Dream by acting as a critic, guide, and sponsor who shares the Dream and encourages its development.

She also serves to support the man's break with his dependency on his parents and to stimulate and bring out his sexual, romantic, and affectionate feelings. This type of special relationship is seen as important to both men and women (Special Man), and when it occurs within the context of marriage, it is crucial that both partners' dreams are supported, or future tension and disillusionment in the relationship can occur.

The Age Thirty Transition follows between the ages of 28 and 33. Levinson saw it as "one of nature's ingenious devices for permitting growth and redirection in our lives" (Levinson 1977, p. 103). It is a time when previous commitments are questioned or new, strong ones are made for the first time. During this stage the old life structure can be reworked, leading to a more satisfying, enriched life pattern. For some this can be a smooth, gratifying period; for others it is a profound crisis. Marriages became threatened, divorce seemed to peak, and work roles often shifted for the sample studied. It is a crucial time in which sound choices can result in a solid foundation for future life periods. The essence of this period is a "growing sense that change must be made soon; otherwise, one will become locked into—and out of—commitments that will become more and more difficult to change" (Kimmel 1980, p. 99).

The final stage of young adulthood is called the Settling Down Period, which lasts from ages 33 to 40 and is marked by the establishment of deeper commitments to work, family ideals, and values. The second stable life structure has been established and is carried through this phase. At this time people make central choices about goals and decisions about what is important in life. The major goals of this period are to establish a niche in society and to work at "making it," which Levinson saw broadly as attaining valued goals. He viewed this phase as a ladder that represents all dimensions of advancement, and progress during this period is marked by the sense of accomplishment in the climb. The culmination of this period is a distinctive phase called "Becoming One's Own Man." It is characterized by seeking the full sense of independence, affirmation, and respect that represents becoming a full and complete man. However, with this respect comes authority and responsibility that forces the individual to give up more of the little boy within. It is a time of conflict and searching, the period when a break with the Mentor typically occurs. This period can be settled by advancement within a stable life structure, by failure and decline within a stable life structure, or by a change in life structures (there are many variations on these). However this period is resolved, it appears to end the time of young adulthood and usher in the advance of midlife.

The Grant study (Vaillant 1977), which included only men, does not break the adult life cycle into as many clear stages as Levinson did. Instead, it discusses general issues that seem to be focused on during broad age periods and supports this with statistics and examples from the men studied. During their 20s and 30s most of the men were concerned with issues of autonomy, career consolidation, marriage, raising a family, and deepening friendships. In fact, marriage appeared to be an important factor that had a relationship to later outcome and success. At age 47, of those men considered to have had the best adjustment, 93% had been married before the age of 30 and were still involved in these marriages at the age of 50. Of those considered to have had the worst outcome, 75% had married after the age of 30 or had separated before the age of 50. It appeared that the majority of the best marriages were entered into between the ages of 23 and 29. During their 20s and 30s, the subjects' primary concern seemed to be with their careers and with competition with others in their field. Some men did have mentors, but this was not typically the case. However, for those who did, this relationship did seem to facilitate their careers. The original goal of this study was to be able to predict from early adult information who would have better adjustment outcomes in later years. However, this goal was not reached because of the wide variability in outcomes.

Between the ages of 25 and 35 these men were focused on their careers and tended to be devoted to their nuclear families. They seemed to sacrifice play for work and did not question their marriages or careers. They tended to forge ahead in their lives in fairly competitive ways. These men continued in this general pattern until their 40s, and Vaillant did not report any specific age periods that related to identifiable issues in development. On the whole, this period between 20 and 40 was devoted to issues of career consolidation and intimacy. In terms of self-judgment, these men saw the years between 21 and 35 as the worst years of their lives and the later years (between 35 and 49) as the best. Sheehy (1976) reported similar conclusions about this whole period. The early years of the 20s are typically marked by a great deal of change and turmoil, with little realization that this change is necessary or inevitable. She saw this time of early adulthood as having marked periods of ups and downs for married couples. Couples experience a great deal of growth, but it tends to be quite uneven, with alternations between growth and stability at different times for each of the partners. Sheehy called the period of the 30s one of "rooting and extending," with the primary focus on buying a home and climbing a career ladder. There is a continued focus on child rearing, a retreat within the family, and some increase in marital dissatisfaction.

Gould (1978) broke the adult life cycle into a number of age stages comparable to Levinson's. Each stage involves a childhood misconception that must be given up and specific tasks that must be performed. Between the ages of 18 and 22 individuals are partially out of their families and continue to complete this task. Through this period people must face the realities that trying is often not enough to accomplish something or be rewarded for it and that working diligently does not always bring success. He characterized this period by the feeling that "I'm nobody's baby now" and by the giving up of the fantasy that if things go badly, then one's parents will be available to set things right. Between the ages of 22 and 28 individuals become established in a chosen life-style that is independent of their parents. They pursue immediate goals related to work and family and are not typically prone to introspection. The major false assumption at this time is that "I'll always belong to my parents and believe in their world." During this period there is a basic concern with independence and separateness in terms of life-style, emotions, and values. Gould considered many marriages that occur during this time to be representative of these issues: The marital partner became important in helping to break away from parents and gain independence. He saw these marriages as failing in the long run because they tended to foster greater dependency within the new relationship.

Through the mid-30s there is a continuation of this family and career process; a central change involves the individual's questioning his or her situation and a growing expansion of awareness of the inner life. This period may begin with uncomfortable or depressive feelings, as the individual becomes aware of feelings, goals, interests, and talents that had been previously hidden. However, these issues do become accepted and tend to lead to a different perspective on the world that is valuable for growth. At this point the basic misconception that must be dealt with is that "life is simple and controllable." In conjunction with this is the realization that the individual must exist in a contradictory world and face contradictions and competing forces within the self. Gould saw this as the end of young adulthood, followed by a long period (ages 35 to 45) of midlife transition (see Chapter 3).

FAMILY LIFE

The family is one of the two areas of involvement (work is the other) for most people throughout the life cycle. Throughout periods and events in life, there is an ongoing interaction between the individual and the family. In fact, the family as a unit or system has a developmental cycle that overlaps and corresponds to the individual's cycle. Adults experience an orderly progression from an unattached or single stage, to marriage, to childbirth, to their children's adolescence, and to their children's moving out on their own. Although there can be disruptions of this pattern following divorce or unexpected deaths as well as through choosing alternative life-styles, this sequence still appears to be the norm. Throughout the family's life history the central family process involves continued changes in the nature of the relationships in order to support both the needs of the family as a whole and the independent needs of the individual members. This takes place through the expansion, contraction, and realignment of the relationship systems to support the entry, exit, and ongoing development of the family members.

Unattached Adults

This period, which is typically between the ages of 18 and 30, follows one of the most difficult phases of the life cycle, adolescence. The adolescent must begin to sever emotional ties to his or her parents in order to develop a separate emotional identity. This task allows progress to be made toward full life responsibility, launching a career, and relating intimately with others. The separation that takes place through this young adult period must allow room for intimacy to continue while independence is developed. How the separation takes place and is resolved can be a primary factor in the growth of later intimate relationships throughout the life cycle. This is a cornerstone phase in which people formulate personal goals and develop and establish a sense of themselves before uniting with someone else in a new family. It appears that the more adequately adults can differentiate themselves at this time, the fewer later stresses they experience (Meyer 1980). The success of subsequent marriage is related to the degree of solid personal identity achieved during this period of separation and experimentation. Depending on the resolution to this period, the individual may be capable of fully intimate relationships while maintaining a sense of self and separate pursuits and interests. However, if resolution is not adequate, then the individual may be emotionally dependent or rebellious, for example, and withhold from relationships or become intensely involved with others to the detriment of individual needs (Carter and McGoldrick 1980).

Marriage

Entering into a formal relationship and becoming part of a couple is an extremely complex and difficult transition; however, it is typically seen as something that is easy and joyous. Traditionally, marriage is seen as an end or solution to many previous problems (e.g., loneliness, extended family difficulties) as well as the culmination of adolescence and the beginning of adulthood. It is marked by the acceptance of one's role in society. Marriage requires that a couple negotiate a variety of personal issues that have been defined previously through each individual's independent status or by parents. In conjunction with forming their own relationship, the couple must develop new types of relationships with friends and family that accommodate their new status as well as maintain their sense of individuality.

During the early stages of marriage the thrust of the relationship is on continued development of intimacy, and the nature of the partners' involvement with each other can be crucial. Couple involvement can be categorized as minimal, limited, or maximal, and although the nature of the involvement may change throughout the family cycle, it is important to the stability and satisfaction of the marriage. Sheehy (1976) saw the newly married couple involved in multiple joint activities, often to the exclusion of others. This exclusiveness may allow directed attention to family development, job success, and building of the relationship, but it also cuts the couple off from contact and support from others. Campbell (1975) reported that on the whole both men and women see the early years of marriage as the best and that women are typically relieved and joyous at this point.

Despite cultural and social changes, marriage is still the primary social bond that people enter into. Most first marriages take place in young adulthood; although the age at marriage has slowly increased over the past decades, men are typically married at 22.9 and women at 20.4 years of age (Glick 1977). Although there was a drop in the rate of marriage in the early 1970s, there appears to be an increasing trend in the number of marriages taking place, and approximately 95–98% of the population marry (Papalia and Olds 1981). Several reports (Kieren, Henton, and Morotz 1975; Troll 1975) indicate that marriages that occur prior to the 20s have the least likelihood of success and those that take place in the late 20s have a much higher success rate.

A variety of research has looked at the role of love in marriage and at the factors that lead to selection of a particular partner. The most important factors seem to involve availability, residential closeness, similarities in background and values, similar social class, and self-resemblance (e.g., in physical appearance, mental and physical health, intellectual abilities). All these factors lead to a balance within the relationship that is important (Barry 1970; Burgess and Wallin 1953; Lopata 1971; Walster and Walster 1978). There is some disagreement concerning the role of romantic love in the decision to marry. Troll and Hieger (1973) found it to be an important reason; Sheehy (1976), on the other hand, saw marriage for love as a myth. She found that couples tend to marry for a variety of more pragmatic reasons—they may feel they should do it (social pressure), they may be trying to find security, to compensate for inadequacies, or to escape home—and that no one (in her study) over 30 reported marrying for love.

In a somewhat different type of study, Neiswender, Birren, and Schaie (1975) examined the characteristics of love and their role in relationships in adolescence, young adulthood, middle age, and old age. They identified six aspects of love and its expression (affective, cognitive, physical, verbal, behavioral, and fantasy) and found that the first four were the most important but that they also seemed to vary in relative importance over the life cycle. Generally, they found that men and women experience love similarly (e.g., men are not more physical or women more emotional), that married love is similar to unmarried love, and that love cuts across all ages (although the experience may be different at different ages). Finally, Walster and Walster (1978) described two types of love that they termed "passionate" and "companionate." The first is what people would call "romantic" love, marked by a strong emotional state with wide fluctuations in feelings. Companionate love is seen as just as deep but less intense and marked by affection and deep attachment. They found that passionate love is short-lived (6 months–2½ years) and that if love lasts it turns to companionate love.

In the most general sense, marriage appears to provide a variety of benefits for those involved: economic advantages, an orderly division of labor, a sense of security, and a sexual outlet. Campbell, Converse, and Rodgers (1976) reported that married people of either sex and at any age report higher happiness than those who are unmarried. However, there do appear to be some important sex differences in marital happiness. Marriage may be more beneficial to men than to women. Although married women report being happier than single women, they appear to be less well adjusted—there is a greater incidence of depression, anxiety, and alcoholism among married than among single women (Bernard 1973). There is general evidence that married people live longer than single people, but this appears to be especially the case for men (Fuchs 1974). Men who have been divorced or widowed seem to experience a greater incidence of diseases that are the result of self-destructive behavior (lung cancer, cirrhosis of the liver), as well as having a higher incidence of accidents, suicides, and homicides, while there is no increase in diseases that are not affected by behavior.

A variety of marital styles have been identified based on psychological and interactional factors. The most important element of today's marital style involves role differentiation and changes in the traditional pattern. Typically, roles have been clearly differentiated. The woman's area of responsibility centered around the home and children, while the husband's involved providing financial support and security and acting as a buffer between the family and the outside world. A great deal has been written concerning changes in this pattern (some of which will be examined in the section on child rearing and work), but a number of authors (Sheehy 1976; Rogers 1979) indicate that the changes have been more in attitudes and values than in actual behavior. The extent to which this is true is somewhat related to social class. It appears that for lower socioeconomic classes and less-educated and older generations a great deal of role differentiation is expected; it takes the form of more traditional marriage roles (Troll 1975).

For those who are middle-class, urbanized, and better educated, there seems to be much more acceptance of role overlap. Earlier studies (Westley and Epstein 1960; Aller 1962; Cutler and Dyer 1965) have indicated that couples with traditional expectations are happier than those with more expressive expectations—possibly because the former can avoid certain areas of conflict that can be triggered by nontraditional roles. Sheehy (1976) felt that both sexes are still "slaves to the traditional shoulds" even though some small changes have been made (dual careers, male interest in children, shared home tasks). She felt that women often have to make a choice about whether to pursue their nurturant needs or their achievement needs. Although changes can be made at various points in the life cycle, there is often a residual effect of the early choice that had been made (e.g., difficulties of late childbirth, limits to late career starts).

Parenthood

In the traditional marriage, having children is seen as fulfilling the relationship and the woman's role. Although there has been a reduction in the number of children in the American family and a delay in having them, most married couples still begin families. Troll (1975) reported that two-thirds of all white mothers have children by the second year of marriage and that three-fourths of all nonwhite mothers have given birth by this time. As in the statistics for marriage, it is clear that from a variety of perspectives the teenage years are the worst for childbirth (Lasswell 1974). This period is marked by a psychological inability to handle both the birth process and the responsibilities of child rearing, a high percentage of still births and birth defects, and a high infant mortality rate. Generally, the years between 21 and 35 have been considered the best years for childbearing. However, the age of first childbirth (in association with age at marriage, the number of second marriages, and the use of contraception) has been increasing. The danger of later childbirth centers around the higher probability of birth defects and infant mortality, but new techniques such as amniocentesis have helped reduce risks. If a couple is at risk for a particular disease, genetic counseling can be helpful in understanding the nature of the risk, assessing probabilities, and monitoring the pregnancy.

The shift from "couplehood" to family involves a major change in roles, attitudes, and values that can have a marked effect on both the individuals and the marital relationship. The addition of a child can disrupt a stable relationship; however, whether this period is actually a crisis for most couples or just a difficult transition is not clear. Several studies (Dyer 1963; LeMaster 1957) indicate that the first birth precipitates a certain level of upheaval; others (Hobbs and Cole 1976; Hobbs and Wimbish 1977) did not find the same level of disruption. Still others (Feldman 1971; Rollins and Galligan 1978) discovered both reactions. Perhaps the goal at this point should be to differentiate the circumstances that lead to a crisis or an adjustment process. Russell (1974) found that the more educated the woman, the more difficulty she had adjusting. Women typically are bothered by fatigue, sleep difficulties, edginess, and emotional upset, while men reported being bothered most by changes in plans, financial matters, and interference of in-laws. The nature of these differences may be related to the role each parent has and the nature of the day-to-day disruptions and responsibilities associated with each. There is some indication that preparation for the new child helps adjustment; however, this appears to be more the case with men than with women (Russell 1974). Another study (Fein 1976) indicated that men who adjusted best had a clear definition of their roles (either as traditional breadwinners or as nontraditional fathers), while those who had the poorest adjustment were ambivalent or uncertain about their roles.

In general, couples with young children feel more stress and pressure than any other group (Rogers 1979). For both sexes, ratings of life satisfaction tend to drop from high to average and remain there until the children leave home (Campbell 1975; Feldman and Feldman 1977). Satisfaction is reported highest for those couples who wanted children a great deal; who could draw on outside resources to help manage time, money, and energy; and who had known each other a long time and were fairly independent as a couple (Rollins and Galligan 1978). Overall, the primary source of conflict for married couples involves differences in child-rearing beliefs (Feldman 1971).

Contraception

The advent of a variety of contraceptive techniques has had a broad effect on the nature and level of sexual activity as well as offering partners control over pregnancy. These techniques have allowed for growing freedom of sexual expression and, for some, have added pressure from peers to engage in sexual activity prematurely. Although contraception is readily available, there are increasing instances of unwanted pregnancies, both within and outside of marriage, that reflect lack of understanding of these methods, disregard for them, insufficient practical education, or psychological conflicts that inhibit their usage. It is likely that health care practitioners will be faced with patients with unwanted pregnancies for whom simply supplying information is not enough to change their contraceptive habits. (See Kolodny, Masters, and Johnson [1979] for a complete discussion of current methods and their medical and psychological side effects.)

Descriptions of contraceptive users and nonusers have been somewhat broad and general. Effective users have been described as mature, independent, self-reliant, secure, ambitious, decisive, and intelligent. They are willing to assume responsibility, establish long-range goals, control their impulses, complete tasks, and tolerate frustration. On the other hand, nonusers are characterized as immature, dependent, insecure, impulsive, and indecisive. They seem to have little desire to control their own lives and to have difficulty in assuming responsibility, tolerating frustration, and setting long-range goals. These descriptions typically refer to the idealized user and the most blatant nonuser; however, there are few people who never use contraceptive methods. More typical and complex are sporadic users (Sandberg 1975). The use or nonuse of contraception is very often situationally determined and varies with such factors as the couple's age, stage of life, experience, mood, and emotional attachment; recent events; and the frequency, setting, and time of intercourse. To understand a particular incident of misuse, a variety of factors must be taken into consideration. Sporadic usage should not be considered abnormal, and an understanding of the reasons for it can help prevent unwanted pregnancies.

Perhaps the most prevalent reason for nonuse involves a current opportunity for intercourse and an unwillingness to put it off. For others, there may be some unwillingness to acknowledge the reality of possible pregnancy or the effectiveness of contraception. Risking pregnancy, in some circumstances, may be seen as a romantic demonstration of love for the partner or a feeling that actively preventing pregnancy would take something away from the relationship and one's sense of giving. Lack of use can also be related to feelings of guilt at being sexually available or prepared, which may represent something immoral to the user. Some people may feel embarrassed about their lack of knowledge about contraception or sexuality in general and be unable to discuss this issue with their family or health care provider. Sensitivity to this difficulty is necessary, and providing information may be an effective mechanism for creating a change in usage. Nonuse, by either males or females, can be related to issues of control within the relationship or of sexual identity conflicts that result in proving one's femininity or masculinity; it may be an expression of hostility by one partner toward the other, of masochism that gets acted out through pregnancy and abortion, of self-indulgence, or of a wish to entrap. As this list indicates, there are numerous complex and interactive reasons for contraceptive nonuse, and it is important to understand the patient and his or her sexual situation as completely as possible in order to effect any change in these habits. It is also clear that since contraception is volitional it can be difficult to make changes in its usage; however, for all patients a starting place is in providing the most complete information while allowing patients to make choices where appropriate.

Pregnancy

The period of pregnancy is a time of great change for couples, with both joyous expectations and fears being triggered. The pregnant woman experiences radical hormonal changes; these can interact with psychological factors to produce dramatic changes in mood. There is some evidence that pregnancy produces a sense of well-being and contentment, but results are conflicting (Hyde and Rosenberg 1976). Positive moods may be related to hormonal changes, but other studies report that the period of pregnancy may be one of tension and crisis or at least be characterized by moodiness and emotional lability (Schuster and Ashburn 1980). The interaction between psychological and hormonal variables that affect mood and behavior during pregnancy may vary with the trimester. Fatigue, vomiting, and headaches appear to be more common in the first trimester; the later months of pregnancy may be characterized by more tension; and there may be a reduction of symptoms in the midphase. Psychological variables, such as the level of identity and fulfillment that motherhood provides, degree of desire for a child, disruption of other life events, and fear about child rearing and responsibility, are some of the factors that may have an effect on the pregnant woman's comfort and the changes that take place during pregnancy (Hyde and Rosenberg 1976).

Schuster and Ashburn (1980) reviewed some of the effects of pregnancy on the husband. Most expectant fathers report that the pregnancy and the expectation of having a child touch on diverse aspects of their lives. While the pregnancy raises questions and fears about responsibility and financial security it also seems to be marked by strong feelings of pride. Schuster and Ashburn described a study that has identified three basic orientations of men that influence their response and involvement in their wives' pregnancies. The man with a romantic orientation may experience this period as quite difficult and have trouble adapting and making changes in his roles and responsibilities. The career-oriented man may resent the pregnancy and feel it as an intrusion on his life-style and current activities. There may be a tendency to resist necessary changes and to remain detached throughout the process. The family-oriented man seems to accept the pregnancy and sees fatherhood as a fulfilling goal. He is generally involved during this period, and the partners often establish a closer bond and increased intimacy. Regardless of orientation, many men feel that they lose their own identities as more and more attention is paid to their wives.

An important factor during the course of the pregnancy that greatly affects the marital relationship is the expression of sexuality and affection. The continuation of sexual activity is sanctioned in our society, and few restrictions are placed on it except during the first four weeks after delivery. Many couples still maintain fears that sexual intercourse will be harmful to the fetus, believing that orgasm may produce a miscarriage, that infection may occur, or that intercourse is inherently uncomfortable during this period. It is often necessary for health care providers to discuss these concerns and educate expectant couples about sexual activity; however, usually the couple is just informed that intercourse is not prohibited and that they should proceed as they see fit. This type of instruction typically does not resolve the couple's questions, and often more explicit information (e.g., about positions) is needed. Typically, throughout the pregnancy there is a general decline in the woman's sexual interest, although during the second trimester women do report an increase in sexual tension and activity. Sexuality is important during this period, but there is some evidence that women experience strong affectional needs during pregnancy that can be fulfilled through nonsexual physical contact. The level and nature of the couple's interaction during pregnancy is tied to their preexisting relationship as well as their individual comfort and discomfort with the thought of the expected child and the changes that will occur (Kolodny, Masters, and Johnson 1979; Schuster 1980).

Infertility

Infertility is diagnosed when a couple has not been able to conceive after a year of trying without contraception; it affects about 10–15% of the population. The average time for conception to occur is 5.3 months and, typically, 25% conceive after one month, 63% after six months, and 80% after a year (Kolodny, Masters, and Johnson 1979). Fertility problems appear to be related to male problems in approximately one-third of the cases, to female problems in one-third, and to joint problems in one-third. Psychologically, infertility has a profound effect on both partners' sense of identity, feelings of control over their lives, sense of helplessness, and future sexual interactions. It can serve as an extreme stressor in the relationship throughout the process of seeking help, which can often be very frustrating (Schuster 1980). Couples often face many misunderstandings about infertility that can lead to conflicts. They may also become so preoccupied with their task that many other aspects of closeness and intimacy are ignored. This may lead to distance and tension in the relationship, which can in turn have an effect on conception.

Initially, infertility counseling involves exploring the couple's sexual relationship and establishing whether penetration takes place during intercourse, whether douching is used that can kill sperm, and if there are related sexual problems such as impotence or vaginismus. Next, an evaluation of the male's sperm may lead to dietary changes, prohibition of alcohol consumption, or an assessment of heat-related factors that can affect sperm life. It must be ascertained whether the woman is ovulating or if there is a blockage of the fallopian tubes. There may also be joint problems, such as a unique antigen-antibody reaction that kills the sperm or misunderstandings about spermatogenesis that lead the couple to avoid intercourse to save up sperm. This results in sperm death, as sperm cannot survive more than 3 weeks of storage. Finally, infertility can be related to psychological factors that include a fear of pregnancy, other more personal and idiosyncratic fears, or an expression of hostility or ambivalence. There is evidence that a large percentage of infertile couples can be cured; however, when this is not possible, consideration of such options as adoption or artificial insemination may be appropriate, as well as helping the couple to deal with the psychological impact of their inability to conceive (Kolodny, Masters, and Johnson 1979; Schuster 1980).

Abortion

The topic of abortion is a highly emotional one that involves the social, cultural, religious, political, and legal spheres. Currently, there is little clear information about the effects of induced abortion, and what information is available is often biased by the investigator's own perspectives. Three primary areas need to be evaluated: the immediate psychological effects, the long-term effects, and the effects of unwanted children on those denied abortion. There is general agreement that the most immediate psychological reaction to abortion is relief; this is especially true for women who receive early abortions and have not developed an attachment to the fetus. The greater the attachment, the more difficult the process. It is also true that the later the abortion takes place, the more risk is involved. A large number of studies show that the most common post-abortion psychiatric finding is guilt, but this finding is challenged by a variety of studies that indicate an absence of any psychiatric problems following abortion. Perhaps the clearest thing that can be said at this time is that the woman who is most psychologically vulnerable prior to the procedure is the most likely to experience negative effects afterward. There is little information concerning the long-term consequences of this procedure, but a few studies indicate that children born to women who were denied abortion have more difficulties than others (reviewed in Babikian 1975). It would appear that those women who do have difficulties had conflicts over the pregnancy, lacked support from their partner or others, and may be left with a fear of pregnancy that can affect their subsequent sex life. There is also some evidence that women who have had vaginal abortions with cervical dilation have twice as high a risk of losing subsequent fetuses as well as a higher risk of premature birth and perinatal death (Schuster 1980).

Alternative Life-Styles

Since 1970 a great deal has been written about alternatives to the traditional married life-style, and a variety of approaches have developed among small segments of the population. These include open marriage, extended single living, homosexual adaptations, and cohabitation in a variety of forms. As these styles become more generally acknowledged, it is likely that research will begin to explore the levels of happiness, adjustment, and sources of difficulties in these life-styles and the details on who selects particular life-styles. There has been an increase in the number of people living singly that seems to be due to the later age of marriage, increased divorce, and choice of a single life. Between 1970 and 1975 the numbers of adults between the ages of 25 and 34 who had never been married increased by 50% (Papalia and Olds 1981), and among those aged 20 to 34, 25% were single. The choice of this life-style appears to relate to issues of freedom, independence, and flexibility as well as changes in social norms that accept singlehood in both men and women. Historically singlehood has been more accepted in men, but women's ability to pursue careers and build economic independence has brought about a great change in their status. Specifically, limited research has shown that women are less likely to marry if they are past 30 without having previously been married. By this time, as men have done, they have become invested in their careers and have built social and professional lives that meet their needs for achievement, affiliation, and identity. In fact, single women are reported to be better adjusted and happier than single men (Schwartz 1976).

As with the choice of singlehood, between 1970 and 1978 the number of couples cohabiting doubled. In 1979 it reached 1.1 million (Papalia and Olds 1981). Kimmel (1980) reported on research indicating that most college-age couples see cohabitation as a step toward marriage rather than as a separate, permanent life-style. Papalia and Olds (1981) reported that most of those relationships (63%) last less than 2 years before marriage or ending takes place. Jacques and Chason (1979) found no relationship between cohabitation and eventual marital adjustment. It appears that this type of relationship involves many of the issues of marriage (e.g., overinvolvement with another, sexual adjustments, possible loss of personal identity, overdependence) as well as other problems inherent in this life-style (ambiguity, jealousy, and desire for commitment). Other types of cohabitation life-styles include a variety of communal arrangements as well as variations on the traditional marriage. These can range from monogamous relationships with contracts of responsibilities and freedoms to open arrangements between couples or within communes for free social and sexual exploration. All these forms can make up part of the homosexual life-style, and it is important not to stereotype either the type of relationship or those involved. Any extensive discussion of these life-styles and the social changes that have allowed them and have been implemented by them is beyond the scope of this monograph. However, it is important for health care professionals to be aware of the multiple living arrangements that currently exist. This can foster understanding of the social elements of patients' lives as well as the possible stresses and strains that can affect the development of numerous mental disorders and recovery and adjustment to chronic problems (e.g., availability of social supports and the effects of disability on life-style).

Divorce

There is a growing population of separated and divorced individuals as a result of a variety of social and personal issues (acceptability of divorce, expectations of marriage, increased demands on marital partners, etc.). The increase in divorce is most evident in young adulthood, although there has also been an increase in middle and later life. Divorce is more likely in the early years of marriage, in childless marriages, among those who marry young, and among those coming from unhappy parental marriages (Kimmel 1980). The process of divorce is often quite painful to those involved, and according to Feldberg and Kohen (1976), divorce is typically caused by problematic situations rather than personal deficiencies and incompatibility. Regardless of the nature or outcome of the divorce, a difficult period of adjustment always follows. It involves establishing new roles and status, experiencing wide ranges of emotions, and establishing new social systems and relationships to ex-spouse, children, parents, and friends.

Bohannan (1975) delineated six separations that take place during the process of divorce. *Psychic divorce* involves the renunciation of the spouse and is accompanied by a period of mourning. *Legal divorce* involves the actual dissolution of the marriage through the court system. In the past this process has been adversarial, but more recently it has shifted toward concepts of incompatibility, irretrievable breakdown, and ultimately, in some states, to no-fault divorce. *Economic divorce* involves the redistribution of the goods acquired during the marriage. This is often a source of great conflict for couples and leads to the reemergence of angry feelings. It also has implications for postdivorce adjustment in terms of finances and the degree of loss and separation from possessions that have been important in the lives of the divorcing couple. *Community divorce* is concerned with separation from parts of the extensive social network that couples establish. It may involve giving up in-laws who have been important and friends who may continue with one or another of the divorcing spouses. These changes can initiate feelings of loneliness and isolation as well as trigger a great many anxieties about establishing new relationships.

Coparental divorce reflects the changes that must take place in child rearing and the development of single-parent status. The final stage involves the *separation from dependency,* the achievement of a state of autonomy that was often lacking within a dependent marriage. This step may be the most difficult and frightening to achieve and is often avoided through remarriage shortly after the divorce.

Divorce results in fairly dramatic changes in life-style as well as in the sense of self. For those with children, the task of being a single parent may be one of the most demanding, especially trying to balance one's own needs with those of the child. Within this situation there are financial issues; feelings of anger, failure, loneliness, and being trapped; conflicting demands; and lack of time. The greatest difficulty for single mothers centers around employment and finances; single fathers have the greatest difficulty with child care (Kimmel 1980). Despite the increase in divorce, most people tend to remarry; however, there is currently no clear-cut data about the factors that contribute to the success of second marriages. Remarriage leads to additions onto the extended family system, with a variety of satisfactions and problems (e.g., loyalties, guilt) inherent in this. However, there is evidence that there is no difference in happiness or adjustment between children brought up by either natural parents or stepparents (Bohannan and Erickson 1978; Wilson, Zurcher, McAdams, and Curtis 1975). The whole process of divorce, from the initial phases of realizing dissatisfaction through the actual event and the later adjustment period, is a time of fluctuating strains, stresses, and tensions that can have profound implications on health and health care–seeking behavior. Divorce is an idiosyncratic transition that is not a typical part of the life cycle. Nor is it predictable, and as discussed in Chapter 1, this type of event has more extreme implications for health and life-style than other, more predictable transitions.

WORK

The other primary area of involvement for adults is work, which is the focus of an enormous investment of time, energy, and commitment. As the individual develops a work role, it adds to and helps resolve identity issues that have continued from adolescence and becomes one of the focal points for generativity and integrity issues. Throughout the life cycle there is an ongoing interaction between family and work that can result in either conflict or satisfaction. These two primary life spheres can reinforce, hinder, or balance each other in terms of the individual's derived satisfaction. One of the signs of adulthood in our culture is getting a job, and although this can often be delayed by continued training and education, it still marks the early transition from adolescence to young adulthood.

However, the process of career choice begins before this period. Super (1957) delineated five stages for career development that start with a *crystallization* period between the ages of 14 and 18. During this time the adolescent begins to develop some awareness of possible choices and may even experiment somewhat in related fields or in finding information from books or other people who may serve as role models. Following this is a period of *specialization* (18–21), which consists of job training either through work in a field or continued education. Then, there is a period of *implementation* (21–24), in which an entry-level position is gained, followed by a *stabilization* period (25–33), in which the individual becomes established in the field. From the age of 35 on, there is a *consolidation* period of work involvement and growth.

Beginning this process of involvement is often difficult, and the first year of a job is a critical period. The young adult is initiated into the general work force as well as into the specific position and must face fears about competence and self-worth. A variety of factors, many of which operated prior to the actual period of job selection, affect choice of occupation. Such background factors as socioeconomic status, ethnic origin, intellectual level, sex, and race all interact to establish a range of occupational choices for each individual (Kimmel 1980). For many it is difficult to go beyond this range. Some can achieve more, often through an unusual or "critical" experience or through identification with a role model in a different occupation. Stockmal (cited in Papalia and Olds 1981) discussed the "critical event," which he felt is a major factor in job choice. This can involve a chance meeting, luck, a personal experience, a major tragedy, or any unexpected event that leads to a career choice or opportunity. Other factors that influence job selection are identification with someone in a particular field; a meaningful experience related to a particular occupation; particular interests, talents, or abilities; and particular personality features.

Once people enter a particular field, they must confront the realities of the job. These include inconsistencies between their expectations and the actual demands of the job and their role in it. They must also find a way of integrating their work and personal roles, which often requires a shift in their sense of self. Havighurst (1965) described two work attitudes that are commonly seen: (1) The "society maintaining" work attitude, which is characterized by a lack of satisfaction and interest in work, with the primary motivation being the paycheck; and (2) the "ego involving" attitude, which is marked by a great degree of satisfaction and derivation of self-respect and self-worth, from which prestige, social participation, and creative expression follow. Adjustment to a particular job appears to be related to such factors as whether the job allows a desired role, whether it effectively utilizes ability and training, how the individual reacts to authority, and what level of advancement (pay raises and responsibility) is available (Hurlock 1980). It appears that the nature of adjustment, using Havighurst's criteria, is closely related to the type of job. Several studies (cited in Troll 1975) indicate that the higher the prestige of a particular job the more intrinsic factors play a part in adjustment and satisfaction, while the lower the job prestige the more extrinsic factors are important. Other reports indicate that although overall most workers find intrinsic rewards more important than extrinsic, blue-collar workers rate pay more important (Troll 1975).

A number of studies have evaluated job satisfaction, and there is a general view that workers are satisfied with what they do. A 1974 survey (Quinn, Staines, and McCullough 1974) found that 75% of those under 21 were satisfied, 84% in their 20s were satisfied, and of those over 30, 90% reported satisfaction. Wilson and Wise (1975) surveyed 300,000 workers who were approximately 30 years old and found that 80% were satisfied and only 8% wanted to change jobs. Finally, a 1977 study (Quinn and Staines 1978) indicated an overall drop in worker satisfaction compared to past studies that focused on discontent with pay, fringe benefits, and promotions. A further breakdown of this data indicated that men were less satisfied than women, blue-collar workers were less satisfied than professionals, and technical people and salaried workers were less satisfied than the self-employed. Another difference from the past concerned how people's jobs fitted into their overall lives. There seemed to be a shift from direct concern with the job to concern with how it was incorporated into other aspects of life and whether it enhanced or hindered a total life-style.

Satisfaction is an issue in job stability and variations in career mobility. As Kimmel (1980) noted, there has been an assumption that people typically make a decision about a career and then maintain it throughout their lifetimes. However, this does not appear to be the case. There is evidence that about 75% of all workers change careers at some point. This is less true for professionals and highly trained technicians. The typical change involves an upward move, which does not appear to be related to whether the change was voluntary or involuntary. The same pattern appears to occur for both middle-aged and younger workers. Although career changes take place at various points, there appear to be several styles of work pursuit. About 30% of all workers tend to pursue their careers in a hierarchical progression (Wilensky 1961). For the majority of workers, however, there is a disorderly history marked by a lack of pattern to the sequence of jobs. Finally, there is a third type that is seen as an orderly career with a sudden shift at some point.

Working Women

Although women have long worked outside the home, there have been important changes in this phenomenon since about 1950. Between 1900 and 1940, 20% of all women 14 years or older worked; however, working women were characteristically young, single, and poor and typically terminated work after marriage or childbirth (Huston-Stein and Higgins-Trenk 1978). It has also been more likely that black women would be employed than white; this has been the case regardless of educational level. Since 1940, there has been a steady increase in the number of white married women who work, and since 1970, more than half the women who were married and had school-age children were working. Historically, this process began with middle-aged women working in the 1950s, and during the 1970s those with preschool children increasingly entered the work force (Hoffman 1979). In conjunction with this pattern, women have become more involved in continuous employment rather than in interrupted work. They are no longer taking the years of child rearing away from work but tend to return to work at earlier phases of child rearing. Continuous employment seems to be more common for well-educated women; a 1970 survey (cited by Huston-Stein and Higgins-Trenk 1978) reported that of women with college degrees 56% were working, of those with more advanced training 71% were working, while of those with less than 8 years of schooling only 31% worked. Another study indicated that women with more education tended to be working more consistently 7 years after their education was completed than those with less education (Wells 1966).

There are a variety of reasons for the increasing employment among women. There are more single women in early adulthood; women are marrying later; they remain childless for longer periods of time; their educational level has increased; there have been changes in discriminatory practices; support systems have become available; and the divorce rate has increased, which provides an impetus for growing self-sufficiency. Although employment possibilities have opened up at all occupational levels and women have increasingly begun to enter the professions, the greatest increase in employment appears to be in low-status, poorly paid, clerical types of positions. There are consistent pay differentials between working men and women. In 1974 the median income for males was $11,835; for women it was $6,772. By 1980 the differential had not changed very much, but it was confounded by the number of years that individuals have been working and the nature of the positions available to them.

Discrimination still operates throughout the work setting in a variety of subtle and direct ways. Van Dusen and Sheldon (1976) indicated that discrimination may affect advancement more than entry into a field. There still is a traditional view that men are the breadwinners and women work only to supplement income; this view subtly increases the male's chances of getting a job and advancing within it. Statistics do not bear out this view. In 1974, three-fifths of all working women were living alone and providing their sole support or their husbands were earning less than $7,000. General stereotypes portray women as having a variety of undesirable characteristics that do not lend themselves to careers. They are seen as emotional, incompetent, inferior, and unable to handle high-level jobs (Herman and Sedlacek 1973; Ross and Walters 1973). This stereotype is often held of women in general and can affect entry into the work force. However, the stereotype often disappears once a woman has demonstrated clear superiority in a particular job or setting. Furthermore, it is extremely difficult for women to integrate home and work life, often because the job world demands excessive commitment in time and energy and does not allow much flexibility. Papanek (1973) found that advancement often requires a helping spouse to handle many of the day-to-day responsibilities. As more men remain single and accept child-care responsibilities, they may find their career development affected as well.

Although many factors that contribute to women's pursuing careers are grounded in childhood socialization and role models (see Billingham 1981), early adulthood seems to be a critical period in career orientation. The crucial factors center on the timing of major life events, such as marriage, childbearing, education, and beginning work. As choices about these events (especially childbirth) are made, future choices become more and more limited. This process works in another way as well: Women who embark on a career without a major commitment can find their involvement growing until that becomes their life focus and excludes other choices. There appears to be a continuity from childhood to adulthood in terms of achievement behavior, and women who are career-oriented tend to exhibit traits that have been considered masculine—aggressiveness, dominance, objectivity, independence, assertiveness, and adventurousness (Bachtold 1973). However, possession of these traits does not mean that they are less feminine or less skilled in marital or maternal roles and behavior (Birnbaum 1975).

In light of sociocultural changes in employment practices, it is evident that women will continue to be a crucial part of the work force on all levels. It is important to briefly examine the impact of their participation in the work force on family life and self-satisfaction. While women increasingly see themselves as oriented toward a career, often in combination with marriage and family, men have a different orientation and perspective. Few men want their wives to work continuously (94–97%, depending on the study), and although 40–60% accept the concept of a career interrupted for child rearing, they do not expect their wives to return to work until after the children have left school. This is in marked contrast to women's expectations, which involve an earlier return to work (Huston-Stein and Higgins-Trenk 1978). These different expectations can be a source of great conflict within a marriage, and the support of her spouse and his orientation toward work are often crucial to a woman's career continuance pattern. As discussed earlier in the section on marriage, although one might expect that in dual-career families the home responsibilities would be more equally divided, this does not appear to be the case. Women typically have primary responsibility for both the home and child rearing (Kreps and Leaper 1976; Robinson 1971). In the Robinson study the employed women spent 3 hours and 40 minutes a day in child- and housecare activities; the employed men spent 1 hour and 15 minutes on those activities. In fact, the major problem for women who work has been related not to role conflicts but to role overload. There is not enough time to adequately meet three roles (career woman, wife, mother) at one time, and there is currently inadequate help with and acceptance of this difficulty.

Two recent review articles examine the role of maternal employment on children and generally conclude that there is no clear evidence that the mother's working outside the home is detrimental to the child's development (Hoffman 1979; Dunlop 1981). Although further investigation is necessary, there is fairly strong evidence that, on a general level, such employment actually has beneficial effects: Children have higher educational aspirations and higher academic achievement (especially in lower-class families); daughters have higher career aspirations; children have less traditional sex-role orientations and are more likely to assume responsibilities for household tasks. These same reviews indicate that day care, depending on the kind and quality of the program, does not interfere with the parent-child bond, nor does it affect the child's intellectual development. The primary factor that does seem to affect children with working mothers appears to be the mother's satisfaction and attitude toward her job. If she is satisfied with her employment, then it is likely that her child's adjustment will be positive. Job satisfaction for women, as for men, is dependent on a variety of interrelated factors. Perhaps the most important factors for women involve the fit between abilities and training and the job itself, the possibility for advancement and leadership roles, and the ability to handle the work overload through a variety of resources.

Despite the stresses inherent in working, there are a variety of benefits for the working woman: personal income, fringe benefits, opportunity to develop skills and abilities, an expanded social network, and a sense of personal satisfaction. Dunlop (1981) summarized a variety of other benefits that have been tentatively shown in the research on women and work. These include fewer psychosomatic symptoms, positive self-concepts and higher levels of esteem, greater satisfaction than nonworking women with what they do, more equitable marital roles in terms of power and decision making, and a greater tendency to enjoy their relationship and activities with their children.

HEALTH CARE

Prevalence of Disease

Young adults can be considered the healthiest subgroup within the population in terms of both objective evaluations and self-ratings of health. Most have outgrown childhood ailments, get sick infrequently, and recover easily from illness, and few have chronic incapacitating conditions (Papalia and Olds 1981). When acute conditions occur, they are typically either respiratory or related to an injury. The most frequent reasons for hospitalization involve childbirth, accidents, and digestive and genito-urinary diseases. There is some evidence that women pay more visits to physicians during this period than men do. This appears to be because of routine gynecological visits as well as women's greater sensitivity to their bodies, which allows them to be aware of symptoms sooner than men are (Papalia and Olds 1981). Although general health is better and the death rate is lower than in any other life stage, there has been a consistent increase in the number of deaths during the late teens and early 20s. At this time of life the death rate for men is triple that for women; this difference is related to the large number of violent deaths. Seventy-five percent of all deaths at this age are caused by accident, homicide, or suicide. It is more likely that whites will die in automobile accidents, while blacks (of either sex) are five times more likely to be murdered; murder is the leading cause of death for blacks (U.S. Department of Health, Education, and Welfare 1979; this source will be used as the basis for the following discussion except where otherwise noted).

Over the past 30 years, there has been a general reduction in the incidence of life-threatening infectious and communicable disease. During midlife the majority of deaths are now caused by such degenerative disorders as heart disease, stroke, and cancer, while for those younger than 40, accidents are the major cause of death. Along with driving and work-related accidents, suicide and homicide are major contributors to the death rate, and very often all these events are associated with alcohol or drug abuse. There has been a continued increase in the level of heavy drinking at all age levels, and although young adults drink less regularly than older adults, they tend to consume more when they do drink. In 1979 the United States had the highest homicide rate in the world; about 70% of these deaths were the result of personal disagreements and conflicts, while only about 30% involved people who were totally unknown to each other. The incidence of these causes of death in young adulthood appears to be related to social factors, errors of judgment, aggressiveness, ambivalence about living, and the propensity for greater risk-taking among the young. This life period also shows a much higher incidence of sexually transmitted diseases than any other. Disorders such as gonorrhea, syphilis, genital herpes, and nonspecific urethritis are commonly seen in young adults by health care providers, and the incidence of these disorders has reached 8–12 million cases a year.

Life-Style and Risk Factors

Perhaps the most important aspect of young adulthood that relates to health care is the life-style pattern that develops during this period. The source of many problems that develop in the midlife period can be traced to young adulthood. Throughout the life span there is a complex interaction between genetic, environmental, and behavioral factors that contributes to the development of chronic disease. There is evidence that 50% of the U.S. mortality rate is closely tied to the behavioral component, which means that individuals may have more control over their physical destiny than has been previously believed. A number of risk factors that can be changed by conscious effort can have a profound effect on health. These factors, which will be briefly discussed below, include smoking, alcohol and drug usage, nutrition, exercise, and stress. For most, patterns that involve these factors develop in early adulthood and persist through the middle years, with changes occurring only during periods of crisis and often not even at those times. The primary role of the health care provider may be in fostering health or life-styles during young adulthood that serve to prevent the later development of disease rather than treating specific disorders themselves. This task can be carried out through careful evaluation of patients' total life-styles, resulting in preventive education and/or specific programs to alter patterns that lead to disease risk. A variety of preliminary programs have shown that changes in smoking and cholesterol levels and the treatment of hypertension can lead to a reduction in the incidence of coronary artery disease. There is also strong evidence that sociocultural groups that prohibit certain behaviors, such as smoking or alcohol, tend to have a lower incidence of cancer; this includes a broad range of cancers, not only those associated with the behaviors prohibited.

Cigarette smoking may be the single most important preventable cause of premature death in the United States. It is generally known that smoking contributes to lung, larynx, and oral cavity cancers and to emphysema and bronchitis; there is also strong evidence that it is associated with blood vessel diseases, stomach ulcers, cancers of the pancreas and urinary bladder, and other minor respiratory infections. Cigarette smokers have a 70% greater risk of death from all causes at any age than nonsmokers, and there is a high incidence of debilitating chronic diseases among those who smoke. Due to the publicity about the connection between smoking and health, there has been a reduction in smoking among males; however, there appears to be an increase in the number of women who are beginning to smoke. There is an increasing number of new smokers among both males and females; this increase appears to begin during late adolescence. Most people who begin smoking are not aware of the increased risk of cardiovascular problems, do not believe that they will actually suffer any harm, and believe that they will smoke for only a limited time. In reality, once smoking begins it is difficult to stop, and there is a high rate of return to smoking for those who have stopped. Although there are a variety of programs to change smoking patterns (e.g., behavioral, hypnotic, and withdrawal methods), their success has been highly variable, and there is evidence that of those who actually quit smoking 95% do it on their own. Often health care providers do not routinely evaluate smoking habits; surveys have indicated that many have not discussed the elimination of smoking with their patients. The termination of smoking can result in important health changes; for example, within 2 years of quitting, the ex-smoker's risk of heart disease returns to what would be expected for that age level.

As noted earlier, alcohol abuse is a major factor in a high percentage of deaths in traffic accidents, homicides, and suicides. Excessive drinking is also associated with the later development of cirrhosis (one of the ten leading causes of death) and cancers of the liver, esophagus, and mouth. The impact of alcoholism is felt throughout our social structure in health and medical costs, lost production, family disruption, accidents, and expenses for treatment programs. The per capita consumption of alcohol rose steadily during the 1960s and 1970s, as did the proportion of heavy drinkers in the population. The same is true of drug usage, which is a major risk factor in young adulthood. The nature of the drugs used is extremely varied; they include many that are prescribed by physicians and are misused or overused, as well as street drugs such as stimulants, depressants, hallucinogens, heroin, marijuana, and cocaine. Depending on the nature of the drug, a wide range of effects are experienced, some of which can be harmful. Some drugs can produce directly life-threatening reactions, but concern more typically involves secondary effects such as accidents, overdoses, and bad combinations of drugs that produce medical emergencies. Changes in social usage patterns and changes through individual treatment programs have been difficult to achieve for drug and alcohol abusers; however, awareness of this issue, education of patients, and appropriate referrals may all be required of the health care practitioner at one time or another.

At this time diseases related to diet deficiencies, other than iron deficiencies in women and children, are rarely seen in practice; however, the incidence of such diseases may vary depending on the subculture being treated. Nutrition is still a major factor in health care, but the focus has shifted from undernourishment to obesity. There is a high level of obesity among middle-aged women in both upper and lower socioeconomic classes, and although the figures for men are lower, it is still a widespread problem. Obesity is associated with diabetes, gallbladder disease, and high blood pressure, and in conjunction with other risk factors it can contribute to heart disease. Dietary patterns have been related to increased risk of cardiovascular disease through levels of serum cholesterol, intake of saturated fats, and salt intake. Diet has also been linked to cancer. Although more research is needed to confirm these preliminary findings, there is some evidence that colon cancer may be related to high consumption of animal fat and low consumption of plant fiber and that hormone-related cancers of the ovaries and prostate may be linked to fat intake as well. In light of the growing body of evidence relating nutrition to disease, information about diet is extremely important as a preventive measure.

Exercise and physical fitness lead to a variety of beneficial physiological and psychological changes. Those who exercise regularly typically report more energy, require less sleep, and sleep more soundly. They also see themselves as less anxious and less depressed and as having higher self-esteem. Physiologically, they have improved muscular strength and flexibility and increased heart efficiency and may have lower risk of developing cardiovascular disease (although this has not been adequately confirmed). Sustained exercise that requires large amounts of oxygen (aerobic) may lower blood pressure in hypertensives, lower serum cholesterol levels while maintaining high-density lipoprotein levels, and eliminate excess weight, all of which are beneficial to health.

Finally, levels of stress and coping strategies are factors that are closely tied to continued adult health. Stress is an inevitable part of life, but there is evidence that excessive stress (what constitutes excessive stress probably varies with the individual) and ineffective coping techniques are risk factors in the development of disease. Although the exact role and nature of the relationships is not clear, there is some evidence of an association between stress and the subsequent development of cardiovascular disease, gastrointestinal disorders, mental illness, suicide, and alcoholism. Stress is discussed more fully in another monograph in this series (Bieliauskas 1981); for our purposes, it is important to recognize that physiological changes (increased blood pressure, heart rate, galvanic skin response, and hormonal output, to mention several) occur during both acute and prolonged stress situations and that these can have serious physical and emotional consequences. Many of the factors that were reviewed in Chapter 1 about adaptation and transitions apply to stress and the individual's effective coping ability.

SUMMARY AND CONCLUSIONS

The period of young adulthood begins with separation from parents and continues until midlife, approximately age 40. During this period a wide range of events influence later aspects of the adult's life. There is typically a progression from living singly, to marriage, to the birth of children while entry into and establishment within the job world occurs. Although there is a traditional sequence and approach to these events, there are also a great many individual differences and alternative life-styles that can make this process more variable and idiosyncratic than it has been in the past. In conjunction with this variability, there are many idiosyncratic or unexpected events that may take place, such as divorce, early death of spouse or child, and job loss, among others, which often precipitate crisis and change in stable life patterns. Researchers have begun to identify the developmental stages of this period and the issues and tasks that seem to dominate each stage. However, this work is currently fairly limited and serves best as a beginning to the identification process. What has become clear is that psychosocial development does not stop at adolescence but continues throughout the life span. This development may be characterized by particular events and related issues rather than by biological and cognitive changes, which marked prior developmental periods.

MIDDLE ADULTHOOD:
AGES 40 THROUGH 65

MIDLIFE CRISIS OR TRANSITION

The midlife transition or crisis has become a common term to explain a variety of behaviors and conflicts that occur in the years of middle adulthood. Although the concept has gained a great deal of public acceptance, especially since *Passages* was published (Sheehy 1976), there has been a great deal of debate and controversy about whether this period is actually a time of crisis. What is more generally accepted is a life stage during which both men and women tend to reexamine their lives, question former goals and achievements, face their mortality, and prepare for the second half of their lives. This period has been described as traumatic, but it may, for many, involve a smooth transition to the next stage of life, allowing a great deal of growth and development. In this section we will explore the studies available that outline the issues and conflicts often encountered at this time and attempt to reach some conclusions about the status of this stage as a crisis point in development.

Levinson (1978) saw the period around the 40-year mark as a link between early and middle adulthood. He proposed that three primary tasks are carried out during this period: (1) reviewing and reappraising the early adult period; (2) modifying any unsatisfying aspects of the previous life structure and beginning to test aspects of a new one; (3) resolving the psychological issues that are introduced by entering the last half of life—forming a new and realistic picture of the self and the world and exploring a number of themes, such as youth versus older age and masculinity versus femininity. Eighty percent of the respondents in Levinson's study felt that this period was a time of either moderate or severe crisis and were actively involved in both internal and external struggles. Many began to question every aspect of themselves and their lives, which led to a great deal of personal upset and turmoil. Levinson felt that this reappraisal, although extremely agonizing, is also a normal part of development. It is necessary because no single life structure can accommodate or permit the realization of all aspects of the self. Also, during midlife, elements of personality that have been previously ignored or suppressed may come to the surface again, pushing for expression and creating conflict.

Gould (1978) identified the period between 35 and 45 as a time of discomfort and reflection for both men and women. Like the other adult periods he has delineated, it is represented by a number of misconceptions that must be faced and resolved. For men the central issue appears to be facing one's mortality: death will eventually be a reality. As this intellectual realization is made, the individual is forced to confront emotional realities as well, because of the deaths of parents and friends. Women appear to be more concerned with issues of independence at this time. They begin to face desires to do things on their own, to seek new experiences, to expand their lives, and to give up the notion that they need to be protected by men. Gould described the overall misconception of this period as "there is no evil or death in the world. The sinister has been destroyed." This misconception has a number of corollary illusions: that safety can last forever; that death cannot strike the self or loved ones; that it is impossible to live without a protector; that there is no life beyond this family; that one is an innocent. As these false childhood assumptions are worked through and let go of, the adult experiences a wide range of feelings associated with a developing sense of vulnerability and the giving up of fears and develops a more comfortable sense of inner-directedness, which prevails from the 50s on. However, this is not achieved without a great deal of turmoil and emotional upset through the period of midlife transition.

Vaillant (1977) reported that the midlife period is characterized by a shift from work and career achievement to inner exploration and a reassessment of earlier life. He saw this period as a stormy one that parallels adolescence in terms of issues, personal discomfort, and uncertainty. It is interesting that for many people, it is in this period that their own children are going through adolescence. Children's adolescence can often serve as a trigger for many parental issues. The adults in Vaillant's study began to reassess their past, break out of felt restrictions, come to terms with suppressed feelings about their parents, reorder attitudes about sexuality, and experience periods of despair, depression, and anger. As Gould (1978) described, as people experience the deaths of those close to them, there is an awakening of feelings of vulnerability but also a feeling of rebirth. Rather than focusing on the fear of these changes, Vaillant emphasized feelings of renewed vigor, excitement, and liberation. Although Vaillant did find that many people make changes during this period, there was little evidence of radical change. Vaillant saw increases in upset and anxiety stemming from the changes taking place, but these increases did not appear troubling to his subjects. Change seems to involve a sense of vigor and challenge, instead of crisis, which he felt has been overdescribed for this period. Despite the troublesome nature of this period, the best-adjusted men in his study considered the years between 35 and 49 to be their happiest time.

A number of other studies have explored the nature of the midlife transition. Nydegger (1976) studied a number of middle-aged men and women of the middle class and found that there was little evidence for seeing this time as a crisis. These subjects reported that they were satisfied with their lives in general and were looking forward to continued satisfaction. Layton and Siegler (1978) found that, although important changes do take place during this period, there was no evidence that crises were more inevitable than at any other life period. What may be more important than identifying the universality of the midlife crisis is identifying the variables that lead to crisis in one individual and growth or easy transition in another. Costa and McCrae (1978) attempted to study specifically midlife crisis in men. They developed a crisis scale that focused on concerns and symptoms identified by Gould. The scale was administered to a group of 315 men aged 33 to 79; the researchers found no differences in focus between age groups and concluded that most men in the study did not experience a midlife crisis. They found no particular age that was specifically identified by the conflicts that were said to characterize midlife. They did find some correlation between focus of concern and certain personality measures, and for those who did report a midlife crisis, it appeared to be associated with long-standing psychological issues.

Livson (1976) studied the midlife period for women by selecting twenty-four women who had rated highest on measures of psychological health in an earlier longitudinal study. They were interviewed at age 50, and the information gathered was compared to the data collected at earlier ages. These women tended to fall into two categories: a stable group who had good psychological health through their 40s and 50s and a group whose psychological health was low in their 40s but improved by their 50s. Those in the stable group were found to adhere to traditional feminine roles and values; those in the second group were seen to be more independent, ambitious, and unconventional (most were involved in careers). It appeared that the unconventional group went through a period of transition and discontent in their 40s, which, although uncomfortable, did not ultimately affect their happiness by their 50s. By that time the issues had been resolved, and happiness and health were comparable to those in the conventional group. This seems to indicate that a key factor leading to the experience of midlife crisis may be the fit between an individual's personality and life-style. As Brimm (1977) suggested, there is currently no confirmation of a universal midlife crisis; however, this period seems to be ripe for difficulties because of the variety of stressful events that may occur. In summary, there appears to be fairly wide acceptance of the components of midlife and of the nature of the transitions that must be made; however, there is not much agreement about whether it should be considered a crisis. Study in this area has just recently begun, and continued research will be necessary to get a clearer picture of adult development at this time.

FAMILY

As described above, the midlife period involves the reassessment of a variety of issues in an individual's life. At the same time, as reevaluation of the past takes place, the individual is confronted with new experiences that require adaptation and adjustment. These include the changing and reorientation of attitudes toward time and its finiteness, the acceptance of the availability of limited options, a redefinition of roles with respect to both parents and children, multiple losses and separations, shifts in the nature of relationships, and an acceptance and recognition of the physical changes that are beginning to take place due to aging. Middle age also provides the basis for new opportunities and experiences that derive from freedoms gained through changes in financial burdens and time constraints. It is a period that can lead to new or renewed satisfactions in activities and within relationships. All these factors have an important impact on and interrelationship with family and marital life. The interaction of these changes with family development requires mutually agreeable modes of adaptation that lead to the maintenance and growth of the relationships involved. This presents a difficult task for most couples, as differences in individual life phases and differences in rate and direction of individual growth are often highlighted and can produce conflict. The manner in which couples and families cope with the stresses of midlife depends not only on the individual histories of the spouses but also on their capacity to cope together and the effectiveness of their problem-solving abilities.

Within the family, parents' midlife typically coincides with the growth of children into adolescence (see Billingham 1981), which eventually leads to the period of launching the children into independent lives. This period is generally when children struggle with separation from their families and the formation of their individual identities. For the adolescent, this time is marked by wide fluctuations in functioning and in the nature and intensity of relationships, by explorations outside the family, and by close identification with peer groups. For the family, this is a period in which constant tests of its structure and flexibility are felt. At the same time a great deal is brought into the family from the adolescent's contacts with the larger world. Both the adolescent and the adult are questioning many aspects of themselves and the world around them, and these processes often interact. Adults may find that their children's behavior conflicts with their own values. This conflict can force parents to reassess their values or create a situation in which they feel caught between the desire to dictate and the fear of alienating their children. Children at this stage can trigger their parents' own sexual fantasies (Levinson 1978), a reemergence of their own adolescent issues that had not been completely resolved, a reemergence of conflicts with their own parents (Ackerman 1980), and a reassessment of their marital relationship as they are faced with the impending loss of children (Papalia and Olds 1981). The family with adolescents is forced to increase the flexibility of its boundaries to allow for the children's independence. This permits adolescents to move in and out of the system, forces the parents' focus away from children and onto their own midlife marital and career issues, and shifts the parents' concern to their own and their parents' aging process (Carter and McGoldrick 1980).

During this period there appears to be a subtle shift in the family constellation; the mother becomes more involved with the adolescent, often as a confidante, and the father becomes less involved than he was in earlier years (Rogers 1979; Sheehy 1976). A number of studies (Rollins and Feldman 1970; Burr 1970; Lowenthal, Thurnher, Chiriboga, and Associates 1975) found that women whose youngest child was in high school were more negative about their marriages than were their husbands. They were also more affected by conflicts with their children, while their husbands felt more stressed by work-related problems. It appears that the women, including those who worked outside the home, focused more on spouse- and child-related problems than the men did. As women are more involved with their children and attuned to them, they seem to be more responsive to adolescent difficulties. If a woman has based her self-esteem on her children, she is more likely to be affected by her child's efforts to separate (Spence and Lonner 1971). Significant stress has been found among women whose children do not adopt parental life-styles or values (Lowenthal, Thurnher, Chiriboga, and Associates 1975). On the whole, the most conflictual area for middle-aged couples involves child rearing (Lowenthal and Chiriboga, 1972).

Launching Children and the "Empty Nest" Syndrome

Following closely after the adolescent phase, the family experiences the independence and loss of children. Historically, the number of years available to couples after the children leave home has increased dramatically; this increase is tied primarily to longer life expectancy (Glick 1977). This period begins with children's leaving but continues through a variety of other changes, including the children's marriages, the birth of grandchildren, the loss of one's own parents, retirement, and other individual changes. McCullough (1980) described a variety of interactive tasks that parents must negotiate during this phase in their life cycle, which can last 20 years. The phase begins with a decreased investment in their caretaking role, which necessitates the acceptance of the children's independence and ultimate separation. This period is often tied to the children's financial solvency, which can fluctuate a great deal over extended periods of time. As children marry, a new sense of family must develop that incorporates both the new spouses and their families into some type of mutually satisfying relationship. As parents let go of their children, the need develops to invest energy and commitment in individual pursuits as well as to reinvest in the marriage. This process may lead to changes in the basic tenets of the relationship, which can result in marital turmoil, extramarital relationships, and/or divorce for many couples. However, if this period is dealt with successfully, spouses can find that such aspects of their lives as work stability, physical comfort, and attainment of mastery through experience and intimacy have been consolidated. As these adjustments take place the midlife couple may make new choices to expand their lives and deepen their interests. At some point in this process, the midlife couple become grandparents (or have to deal with not being grandparents, if their children decide not to become parents), which will again alter the composition and structure of the family and its interrelationships. Finally, during this cycle the middle-aged adult must deal with changing relationships with his or her own parents and face their retirement, disability, increased dependency, and ultimate death.

The loss of children has traditionally been seen as a period of trauma, especially for women. It has been termed the "empty nest" syndrome and has classically been considered a time of depression and despair for women that is linked to the loss of the mothering role (Rubin 1980). This syndrome has been characterized as involving a profound clinical depression with severe psychiatric symptoms, such as despair, sadness, sleeplessness, a variety of somatic complaints, decreased appetite, decreased sexual desire, low self-esteem and self-confidence, a reduction in initiative, and slowing of thinking and motor abilities. The level of distress can be highly variable; however, the presence of some grouping of these symptoms is often taken as evidence of this crisis. A variety of research studies (Bart 1971; Harkins and House 1975; Powell 1977, among others) have documented the presence of this syndrome and the negative effect that child loss has on women. Other studies do not support the existence of this crisis (Deutscher 1969; Neugarten 1974; Neugarten and Datan 1974), yet the "empty nest" remains an accepted explanation of depression in middle-aged women. One of the differences between these two sets of studies is that most of the work that supports the "empty nest" syndrome has been done with women who have been hospitalized for psychiatric reasons, while the work that indicates that it is not a universal experience has been with the general population. It is clear that some women do experience depression related to child and role loss; however, the majority of the data recently reviewed by Rubin (1980) indicate that women in general see the launching of their children as a time of relief that often leads to an increase in both personal and marital satisfaction.

Still, some women do experience loss and subsequent depression. The question this raises is how to identify those who may have problems and the factors that precipitate them. It appears that one factor is how centered the woman's life has been around her children and motherhood (Rogers 1979), as well as the degree of stability and satisfaction derived from other areas of life. Factors such as the length of time children have been gone (Harkins and House 1975), how successful the woman feels as a mother, how she feels about her children as adults (Spence and Lonner 1971), how she has lived life, and how she has prepared for the transition (Powell 1977) all affect the woman's response to this event. Harkins (1978) found that this period was generally not stressful but that things were worse for women whose children did not gain independence. This coincides with findings that child launching is more difficult for working-class than for middle-class mothers (Weissman and Paykel 1974). These differences seem due to the way a child leaves home rather than to the event itself. For most middle-class families this tends to occur at a predictable time (18 years old, when the child goes to college); for the lower classes the time is highly variable and indefinite, leading to a great deal of ambiguity in subsequent role changes. Among those women who have been hospitalized, those with the most difficulty adjusting were disappointed in their children, had an unsatisfactory relationship with their children, and disapproved of their children's life-style. This appears to lead to feelings of self-blame, followed by a depressive episode (Rich 1976; Abramowitz 1977).

There is also evidence that fathers experience distress when their children leave home. In a study by Roberts and Lewis (1981), those who were unhappy were older men who had had fewer children than the other participants. They tended to see themselves as more nurturing than others in the study, yet had poorer marriages. They felt more neglected by their wives, felt that their wives were not sufficiently understanding and empathic, and felt severe loneliness after their children left. Several consistent themes arose from this data concerning the fathers who had difficulties. These men became aware that their marriages and friendships were empty at the same time as their children left home. They had spent their early lives involved primarily in providing financial support for the family, which was no longer needed as much. They had also become more nurturing at a time when their wives and children needed nurturing less because of their growing independence. Rubin (1980) found that men voiced regrets primarily about not having spent as much time with their children as they would have liked. It is likely that this period may have more of an impact on men as they become more involved in child rearing. However, generally, for both men and women, although many do experience feelings of loss and suffering for periods of time, it appears that most are not debilitated by these feelings.

Marital Happiness and Divorce

Reassessment appears to be the hallmark of this period, and it is felt very strongly within the marital relationship. A number of studies have attempted to assess marital satisfaction through the life cycle, with often conflicting results. Pineo (1961) studied adults who had been married up to 20 years and identified a drop in marital satisfaction and intimacy that he labeled "disenchantment." He saw this as a progressive process as one gets further away from the initial marital period when happiness, which had led to the marriage, is typically at its highest. A later report by Burr (1970) challenges this view; it sees marital happiness as rising and falling throughout the relationship. This fluctuation is seen as linked to such specific issues as sex, children, and finances. Sheehy (1976) proposed the concept of the "sexual diamond" which, although it is described in relation to sexual compatibility, represents a variety of behaviors and feelings within a marriage. According to this view, men and women appear to be most similar in terms of their sexual needs and responsiveness in their early 20s and their 60s. Between these ages there is a gradual growing apart that peaks around age 40 and then a gradual growing back together that is complete at around 60. Although this is a hypothetical formulation that has not been researched as yet, it appears to be descriptive of Sheehy's data. Perhaps the most general and accurate statement that can be made about marital happiness at this time is that marriages that have been good up to midlife often continue to grow and develop, while those that have been shaky may become worse as the couple faces the stresses and changes that midlife brings (Papalia and Olds 1981).

As marital dissatisfaction increases and cultural sanctions change, there is an increase in the number of divorces in midlife. Kaslow (1981) reviewed some of the available evidence about the cause and impact of divorce at this time. Divorce is seen by both married and divorced subjects as the life event that imparts the highest level of stress. Late divorce occurs more frequently in traditional marriages than in companionship marriages. The most frequently reported cause of divorce at this time was related to adultery (either multiple incidents over time or a particular incident), and 75% of those divorcing reported long-term unhappiness. Late-divorcing females reported significantly greater increases in independence and self-confidence than males did. More than

50% of the group studied delayed the decision because of their children's ages, and many felt relief as well as stress with the changes the decision led to. Many of the issues that led to divorce and the problems that follow are similar to those discussed in young adulthood. However, several issues are unique to divorce in this period: Life changes have led to changes in the original marital contract that cannot be carried out; individuals have become aware of growing disappointments and unrealized goals that they then decide to pursue; often sexual problems develop and issues of pro-creativity may arise for those who haven't had children or those who have difficulty accepting advancing age; there may be disappointment with children who fail to live up to parents' expectations and spouses who do not provide what was promised; and physical disability may force the confrontation of mortality and role shifts.

Grandparenthood

Typically, at some point during the midlife phase many adults will become grandparents. This event maintains the progression of the family life cycle and bridges a link to the future for adults who are beginning to face their own mortality. Kimmel (1980) reviewed an earlier study by Neugarten and Weinstein that attempted to assess satisfactions and styles of grandparenting. They found that a majority of their subjects felt comfort and derived satisfaction from their roles, although the meaning of the roles seemed to vary a great deal (e.g., biological renewal, emotional self-fulfillment, providing a resource). The study identified five different types of grandparents: the formal grandparent, who leaves primary care to the parents and offers special favors; the surrogate parent; the reservoir of wisdom, who maintains authority; the fun seeker, who has fun with the child but ignores authority issues; and the distant figure, who is not intimately involved with the child except on special occasions. There currently is not a great deal of literature on grandparenting. Issues of the nature of pleasure that is derived as well as the nature of conflicts that may arise through distance, overinvolvement, and authority issues require research. Ethnic and cultural differences in this process also need to be explored more completely to understand how grandparenting fits into the life cycle.

Aging Parents

Throughout young adulthood and often into middle age, the relationship between children and parents, although often reciprocal, still is skewed. Typically, parents give their children financial and emotional support, both for the children themselves and in raising the grandchildren,

and the children accept it. There are continual changes in these relationships, but there appears to be an abrupt change sometime during the
children's middle age when they realize that their parents are aging and
may become physically ill and incapable of caring for themselves, either
partially or completely. Parents who experience a loss of independence
and security, failing health, limitations of social contacts, and decreasing
mobility must face increasing dependency needs that have direct implications for their middle-aged children. Middle-aged children who are confronted with "parenting" their own parents often have a great deal of difficulty. There do not appear to be any explicit roles for this task within our
society, which increases the complexity of the obligation and ambivalence
about fulfilling it.

Rogers (1981) summarized the difficulties of this position. Parents are
forced to contemplate their relationship with their own children, often at a
time when their children are striving for independence and conflicts may
abound. Difficulties within the primary family often develop when siblings
disagree on how to provide care or who should do so. In conjunction with
this problem, there may be an extensive strain on the marital relationship
as conflicts of care, finances, and priorities arise. Weak marital relationships may break under the stress of these problems. It is difficult for people
to observe their parents' loss of health, with possible loss of body control;
this triggers a great many fears of one's own vulnerability and death.
In childhood these fears were comforted and soothed by parents who
are now sick themselves. However, despite these emotional difficulties,
middle-aged children continue to find ways to care for their parents,
and there is little evidence of desertion at this time. Parents and children
tend to live near each other, but most do not live together unless this is
necessitated by illness (Troll, Miller, and Atchley 1979). Support is still not
one-way: Middle-class parents often provide financial help at this time for
their children. In contrast to this, among working-class families it is typically the children who provide aid and support for their parents. The
nature of care for aging parents also changes with social, ethnic, and class
backgrounds; however, when aged parents do need care their families
typically provide it.

Death and Widowhood in Middle Life

Although death and dying will be discussed in the chapters on aging, it
is necessary to at least comment on death in midlife. A chief concern of
women at middle age is the possible death of their husbands (Neugarten
1968). This concern is based in actuarial fact: Women are four times as
likely as men to be widowed, and bereavement is more likely to occur at
an earlier age for women (Walsh 1980). When death of a spouse occurs,

feelings of loss and loneliness often lead to depression, and suicide is not uncommon. This is especially so for men, who have a great deal of difficulty adjusting to the death of a spouse. This period is more difficult for men because social life and family contacts, which the wife typically maintained through the marriage, are generally disrupted. On the other hand, after the initial period of mourning, it appears to be easier for men to remarry and find social contacts; there are typically more women available and men seem to be accepted as single more readily than women. Widowhood for women brings on an extremely difficult period of adjustment that involves giving up the husband as dead; slowly (often over a one-year period) becoming more concerned and involved with the demands of daily living, self-support, and household management; and finally shifting focus to new activities and interest in others (Lopata 1973, 1975). Following death of a spouse, as with divorce, women are often forced into the world outside the home to support themselves and their family—an agonizing process, but one that can result in new feelings of self-confidence and vigor.

WORK

There continues to be an increase in the number of middle-aged workers, as people remain on the job longer before retirement and as more women enter the work force both at middle age and before. There is little information about working women at this time; but for men, midlife is the period of peak status and income and the time when job success reaches its height (Hurlock 1980). Hunt and Hunt (1974) reported that power, wealth, and prestige are controlled and generally concentrated among the middle-aged. In general, attitudes about work shift throughout the life cycle; there is some change at midlife. Workers are concerned with issues of personal fulfillment and satisfaction and consider these factors as important as material success. At the same time, there has been a shift away from obligations to others; responsibility has turned toward the self. Workers may be less afraid of economic insecurity and more willing to take risks in seeking more satisfying positions, but such feelings may fluctuate a great deal with economic conditions (Rogers 1979). These attitudinal changes lead to more emphasis on job satisfaction and less willingness to work at full capacity or remain in a position that does not provide some sense of fulfillment.

In middle age, job satisfaction appears to be related to a number of factors that interact with the general issues being dealt with at that stage in life. Hurlock (1980) summarized the most salient of these as the achievement of goals that had been set earlier, family satisfaction, self-actualization on the job, good relations with coworkers, satisfaction with superiors and coworkers, adequate fringe benefits, security, and the ability to continue working in the same location. For industrial workers the period of the 40s is a critical age for both advancement and level of satisfaction; for those in business and in the professions the critical period comes somewhat later. Typically, across occupations, there is a sharp drop in satisfaction toward the late 60s. This drop also occurs for men about 5 years prior to compulsory retirement (Hurlock 1980), probably because of an awareness that they have reached the highest level of their careers. Although workers do reach their peak in middle age, it still may not coincide with their earlier expectations and wishes. For many people middle age is a period of plateau on the job; advancement has been discontinued, and frustration and disillusionment may mark this time. It is clear that long-term satisfaction is closely related to the job level achieved – the higher the level, the more satisfied workers report being.

During middle age work not only provides an enormous source of satisfaction to men; it can lead to a great deal of stress as well. In middle age there is a high frequency of stress-related illnesses that can profoundly affect working ability; they are often tied to working habits and environment. Some of the stress-related symptoms associated with work are alcoholism, excessive smoking, high serum-cholesterol levels, absenteeism, low self-esteem, increased heart rate and skin resistance, depression, and a greater risk of coronary heart disease. Cooper (1981) reported that workers between the ages of 45 and 64 consult physicians more often and have more restricted activity days than workers between the ages of 15 and 44. In his review, Cooper delineated the job factors that appear to be associated with a variety of stress-related disorders.

Typically, the middle-aged man has made a major commitment to his job and tends to work long hours and take on an excessive amount of work. Two types of work overload have been identified: (1) quantitative, which involves too much work; and (2) qualitative, which involves tasks that are too difficult. Both types of overload can produce a variety of stress-related symptoms, and there appears to be a positive correlation between number of hours worked and later development of coronary heart disease. For many middle-aged workers, the pressure of work overload is not externally imposed but is maintained by an internal sense of pressure. Work role and a lack of clarity about responsibility, expectations, and objectives are factors that are closely linked to low job satisfaction and job-related tension. When the middle-aged man feels torn between conflicting job demands or is forced to do things that he either doesn't want to do or feels are not part of his job, then role conflict is said to be present – again, a source of stress.

There also seems to be a relationship between responsibility for other people, compared to responsibility toward things, and risk of coronary heart disease. It is likely that when responsibilities involve other people, pressure is more extreme, leading to more deadlines and the stress of increased interpersonal difficulties. Workers report increased job pressures if they see their bosses as inconsiderate. The higher they rate bosses in consideration the lower they report job pressure to be. Finally, in terms of the job itself, perhaps the most crucial factor for the middle-aged is career prospects, in terms of both status and the challenges of the job. Issues related to lack of job security and to fears of redundancy, obsolescence, early retirement, and unemployment all can have a profound effect on the worker's health. These effects are also felt by those who are frustrated at having reached a ceiling on their job as well as those who have been promoted beyond their capacities. It is much more difficult to continue job advancement at middle age than when younger; and it may be important at this stage to adapt expectations to new circumstances and seek new sources of satisfaction to avoid the risk of career-related stress and disease.

There is also an area of interface between home and job that can become a source of stress to the middle-aged. Workers must somehow manage their time and commitments so that work and family proceed with as little conflict as possible. The middle-aged man often has few resources available to meet the needs of others after his job commitments are fulfilled. The most typical arrangement to avoid conflict involves a division of labor in which the wife provides support and takes care of day-to-day needs and social ties so that the man can pursue his career. This arrangement, which has been both directly and indirectly supported by business and by our culture as a whole, has been seen as crucial to work success. As more and more women follow full career paths, a number of issues will inevitably arise that will drastically alter this pattern, at least for some workers and employers. Although there is not very much specific research about women involved in full-time careers who reach midlife, a number of books and articles have recently been published that descriptively review many of the issues confronted by dual-career families and the changes that are slowly taking place. The Two-Paycheck Marriage (Bird 1979) and Working Couples (Rapoport and Rapoport 1978) are two of these books. Sullivan and Arms (1981) reported that middle-aged career women have few role models at present; they discussed some of the inventive ways that families and employers are coping with this increasingly common life-style (long-distance marriages, work at home, flexible shifts, permanent part-time employment, job sharing, reduction in job transfers, and relocation and aid in finding employment for both workers). It remains to be seen how this pattern will evolve, and it will be necessary to continue to explore the effects of job-related stress on women as well as men.

LEISURE

Culturally, there have been both a gradual change in orientation toward work – now seen as less central to people's lives than in the past – and a reduction in the number of working hours required to maintain job status. As these changes have occurred, the amount of time not involved in occupational work has increased; this time has to be filled with some sort of activity. Although our society can still be considered work-oriented, there appears to be more acceptance of leisure time as an important element of life-style from which satisfaction and pleasure can be derived. Rogers (1979) described several reasons why leisure is important: It can compensate for the strains of high-pressure living; it can be a source of satisfaction and fulfillment when these are not derived from work or other activities; it can help establish family and social bonds; and it can develop skills and interests that can be carried into later adulthood when retirement occurs and/or more free time is available. Early research made fairly clear-cut distinctions between leisure and work; they were seen as mutually exclusive activities. Leisure was defined as any freely chosen activity not associated with work (Kelly 1972), and the possibility of some form of merger between leisure and work activity was excluded. More recently, Neulinger (as reported in Kimmel 1980) developed a broader conceptualization of leisure, which essentially defines it as a state of mind rather than as a particular type of activity. He identified two factors, each of which is on a continuum – of freedom versus constraint and intrinsic versus extrinsic motivation. These factors interact with each other. What is important in this view is whether the activity is freely chosen and whether it provides a sense of internal satisfaction as opposed to merely external rewards (e.g., salary). In this model work and leisure can merge. This view presents a challenge of identifying and discovering activities that are intrinsically satisfying, can be realistically attempted, and enhance the individual's (and at times others') quality of life. This appears to be a broad view of leisure based on psychological fulfillment that reflects the variety of approaches to life satisfaction within our culture.

Gordon, Gaitz, and Scott (1976) reviewed a good deal of the literature on leisure; their perspective seems closely related to that described above. They identified six major functions or derived satisfactions that people seek through a variety of leisure activities. They saw these functions as representing a hierarchy based on the degree of cognitive, emotional, and physical involvement. In this hierarchy, the more intense the activity, the greater the expenditure of energy and the focused attention it demands and the greater the sensory stimulation it provides. They emphasized, however, that this hierarchy does not reflect the quality or importance of the different activities; it is rather a mechanism of ordering them on the basis of expressive involvement. Each type of activity is important and is probably engaged in at one time or another. They identified (in ascending order) relaxation, which includes sleep, quiet resting, and solitude; diversion, which provides a change of pace and relief from tension or boredom and includes light reading, sedentary hobbies, and social activities; developmental activities, which lead to an increase in knowledge or physical capacity and include new learning, cultural activities, and sustained and focused social activities; creative activities that involve active performance in creating new cultural productions; and finally, sensually transcendent activities, which involve the activation of any of the senses by activities that provide intense levels of pleasure, gratification, excitement, rapture, and joy (e.g., sexual activity, use of psychoactive drugs or alcohol, ecstatic religious experiences, aggression).

Throughout the life cycle leisure is affected by a variety of factors that are current at particular points in time and stem from developmental issues. These factors have been reviewed by Gordon, Gaitz, and Scott (1976). In young adulthood (up to about age 30), leisure is typically influenced by desires for variety, autonomy, and sensory experience. Many leisure activities at this age had been learned from families and school, but other variables, such as occupation, marriage, health status, and monetary resources, contribute as well. Within marriage, shared leisure activities appear to be important in developing a sense of closeness and commitment both between the partners and between parents and children. The 30s to the mid-40s are a period when men are generally involved in their work and traditionally women have been involved at home. Leisure during this time can be seen as intricately tied to the achievement of marital and family growth as well as to the maintenance of individual emotional health. Typically, activities at this stage center around the home and family, with men more inclined toward sports and activities away from the home.

Through this and later life periods, there are some associations between socioeconomic status and leisure. Lower-status people generally engage in relaxing, diverting, or sensually transcendent activities, while higher-status people are involved more in developmental and creative activities as well as less risky sensual transcendence. Financial differences do play a part in this, but there is evidence that class differences do exist.

During the middle years adults face themes that center on changes in their self-concept, issues of control and dignity, and the process of reevaluation and self-acceptance. Leisure can help the adult gain acceptance and warmth from others from activities that differ from those engaged in in the past. It can also help to avoid the feelings of loss and despair that accompany middle age, and it allows the structuring of time when the adult has more time available with less responsibility than previously. Middle age is also a time when couples' leisure activities without their children can foster a renewed sense of intimacy. Activities are less home-oriented and include more evenings out, travel, and an increase in personally expressive forms of leisure (e.g., music, writing, and painting). In later adulthood a key issue is that of maintaining a valued identity after retirement; this can be affected by the nature and quality of leisure activity. A variety of studies indicate that as people grow older, they spend more time in leisure activities, but the range of these activities becomes narrower and they become more sedentary and home-bound. Leisure is a crucial aspect of all life stages; it reflects many of the issues active at specific ages. The nature and level of these activities are important for both immediate and future gratification; the influence of early and mid-life patterns on patterns in later adulthood and retirement is especially important.

MENTAL HEALTH

The most prevalent psychological disorders of the middle-aged are depression and alcoholism; there is also a high incidence of suicide (Boyd and Weissman 1981). For each problem there is a high degree of human misery, substantial morbidity, and some incidence of mortality. Often, people with these problems seek help from primary health care providers; however, their complaints may not always directly express what is disturbing them. For example, someone who is depressed may complain about fatigue, aches and pains, or insomnia, and the health care provider must infer the underlying depression. The same may be true for a variety of psychological problems, and early detection and preventive work can allay a good deal of suffering and prevent unnecessary clinical interventions.

Depression

Depression is a normal human emotion that is experienced by most people at one time or another; it becomes a pathological symptom through intensity, duration, pervasiveness, and interference with normal functioning. The depressive syndrome is characterized by sad mood, loss of energy, sleep disturbance, appetite disturbance, loss of interest, distractibility, low self-esteem, guilt, impaired capacity to perform daily functions, crying, and suicidal ideation. These symptoms can be seen in many combinations, with a wide degree of resultant disruption. The incidence of minor depression in middle age is 3.2% of the population, compared to 1.9% of those younger and 2.7% of those older. The incidence of major depression is 6.3% in the middle-aged compared to 1.9% in young adults (Boyd and Weissman 1981). A number of factors affect the incidence of depression. Women appear to have a higher incidence of depression in middle age than do men (7% versus 2.9%); this difference does not seem to be related to rates of help-seeking behavior, which are often higher for women (Burrows and Dennerstein 1981). This difference in incidence of depression is consistent at all ages, but it is more typical for women than for men to report symptoms related to mood changes, which may make the diagnosis of depression easier or more prevalent for women. Men tend to report symptoms associated with alcoholism; they often do not seek help until hospitalization is necessary. Other symptoms that men tend to focus on include impotence and work difficulties, which can obscure the issue of depression. For women the risk of depression increases up until the early 50s and then begins to decline; for men there is a continued increase in risk of depression throughout adulthood, without any decline in the later years. Factors such as a lack of intimate relationships, grief over a death or other loss, divorce, career problems, and feelings of helplessness can all be precipitants of a depressive disorder. In middle age many changes take place that are associated with these factors, and difficulty in adapting to these changes can lead to psychological disturbances.

Alcoholism

The identification of alcoholism is based on the duration, the amount, and the pattern of drinking; the prevalence and intensity of social problems attributed to drinking; psychological dependence; physiological dependence; and the existence of medical diseases secondary to alcohol intake (liver damage, upper gastrointestinal bleeding, neuropathy, and Wernecke-Korsokoff's syndrome). The incidence of alcoholism in middle age is 4.9% of all men and 3.1% of women (Boyd and Weissman 1981); however, the higher incidence in males may be related to the fact that alcoholism is somewhat harder to detect or recognize in women. Two drinking peaks have been found for both men and women, between the ages of 21 and 24 and 45 and 49 (Mirkin and Meyer 1981). There is some evidence that men begin drinking heavily as teenagers or in their early 20s, while women often do not begin until their 30s; however, medical complications and hospitalizations typically begin to occur in middle age for both sexes (Boyd and Weissman 1981). The incidence is five times higher among nonwhites than among whites, a difference that is also related to social class. It is likely that the effects of heavy drinking are seen sooner in low socioeconomic groups because the physical demands of their jobs mean there is less tolerance and support (higher accident risk, more disruption of motor functioning, for instance). Among the middle-aged, drinking is associated with higher risk for medical problems (including cardiovascular disorders), job absenteeism, job loss, divorce, traffic accidents, and felonies, and at any age, risk of death through accidents, suicide, or medical illness is two to three times higher among alcoholics than among the general population (Boyd and Weissman 1981).

There appear to be two patterns of alcoholism that are related to when heavy drinking begins. For those who can be considered alcoholics in middle age, one group began drinking in young adulthood and continued fairly steadily until the symptoms were recognized. Another group began heavy drinking in their 40s. Those in this group had stable lives until they began drinking in response to some difficulty during middle age, such as depression, bereavement, retirement, loneliness, divorce, or physical illness. For men, treatment is typically sought after a 10-to-15-year history of drinking; it is often precipitated by external events, such as an accident, job difficulty, or medical complication. For women, treatment is sought about 2 years after heavy drinking begins and is often related to marital problems or some complication from a mixture of drugs and alcohol (Mirkin and Meyer 1981).

Suicide

The risk of suicide increases for both sexes in middle age, but men are more vulnerable from this time through later life. Men have a rate of actually committing suicide three times that of women, while women have a rate of threats and unsuccessful attempts three times that of men (Burrows and Dennerstein 1981). Men tend to choose more lethal means of suicide, and suicide is a major cause of death among white, middle-aged males. For men, living alone increases the risk of suicide, and the risk of suicide among divorced or widowed men is five times that of married men (Boyd and Weissman 1981). Suicide risk generally increases with age, with level of depression, and with alcohol consumption and is higher for those with acute or chronic medical illness or chronic pain. Two-thirds of those who attempt or commit suicide have visited a physician within a month of the attempt; this contact is often with a primary care physician. It is crucial that health care providers recognize the risk factors for suicide and carefully explore this issue with patients who may be at risk.

PHYSICAL HEALTH

Healthy People: The Surgeon General's Report (U.S. Department of Health, Education, and Welfare 1979), which will serve as the basis of this section, indicates that 75% of all deaths in middle age are due to heart disease, stroke, and cancer. These are viewed as chronic diseases that have developed through the life cycle as a result of behavioral patterns established in early adulthood; they are slowly progressive and insidious. Other disorders of middle age include respiratory ailments, diabetes, arthritis, rheumatism, digestive disorders, and genitourinary problems (Papalia and Olds 1981). Middle age seems to be a marker for changes in these disorders, increases in symptoms and secondary effects, and increased health care contact; however, many of these disorders developed at an earlier period. As in young adulthood, there are sex differences in health patterns. Men experience more heart disease, digestive disease, emphysema, and injuries; women are more likely to have colitis, gallbladder problems, anemia, diabetes, and varicose veins (Lewis and Lewis 1977). As at other times, men have a higher risk of death, but women are hospitalized more frequently, see the doctor more often, and have a greater number of operations.

Cardiovascular disease poses the greatest risk of death in middle age. It is the leading cause of death for men over 40. Women have a much lower incidence until menopause; at that time their risk begins to increase until it matches the males' at age 85. This group of disorders is responsible for more hospitalization than any other illness, and it is an important cause of midlife disabilities. Throughout adulthood there is a continuous increase in blood pressure levels for those who are hypertensive in young adulthood. This is an important risk factor for coronary artery disease and the most important factor in stroke.

Hypertension affects one person in six; it is more frequent for men up until age 55, when incidence becomes equal for men and women. Incidence among blacks is twice that among whites; hypertension is more frequent in people with lower incomes and education levels. In about 10% of all cases there is a known cause (e.g., kidney disease); in the other cases, termed "essential hypertension," exact causes are unknown. There is evidence that salt intake and stress play a part in its development, but the mechanism of these factors is not yet understood. Hypertension cannot be cured at this time, but it can be adequately controlled through medication, which often must be taken throughout the patient's life. Because there are very few overt symptoms of hypertension, compliance with medical regimens is often a problem that is compounded by frequent adverse side effects of the standard antihypertensive drugs. Behavioral treatments involving restricted salt intake, weight loss, exercise, and relaxation can be helpful by themselves or can augment a drug treatment program.

Both heart disease and stroke are related to the process of atherosclerosis, in which critical arteries become narrowed by fatty deposits consisting of cholesterols and fats. As the artery walls thicken and the arteries narrow, there is a gradual reduction in the amount of blood that reaches various organs. Symptoms typically do not appear until the disease is well advanced, which means that, for most, middle age is the period when its effects are actually experienced. Risk factors include smoking, hypertension, high cholesterol levels, diabetes, obesity, physical inactivity, genetic predisposition, and possibly certain personality characteristics.

The second most common cause of death during this age period is cancer, which is actually a group of diseases with different features and incidences. More than one-third of all deaths due to cancer occur in the middle years; the most common types are lung, intestinal, and breast cancer. As with other disorders of middle age, cancer does not suddenly develop at this time but has begun anywhere from 10 to 25 years earlier, when it could not be detected. A variety of risk factors have been associated with the development of cancer: smoking, alcohol consumption, diet, exposure to radiation and sunlight, occupational exposure to carcinogens, water pollution, air pollution, and heredity. Many of these factors independently increase the chances of developing cancer, and interactions between them can expand the risk enormously. Many deaths due to specific types of cancers could be avoided by limiting exposure to environmental factors and through early detection. Sensitivity to early signs, awareness of a patient's life-style and environment, and an understanding of incidence and risk factors can help both patients and health care providers deal with this problem.

Physical and Psychological Interactions and Health

Within psychology and medicine there is a long history of attempts to identify disorders that could be considered psychosomatic in origin. These were thought to be precipitated and caused by either specific psychological conflicts or psychosocial stresses. They include peptic ulcer, ulcerative colitis, bronchial asthma, rheumatoid arthritis, essential hypertension, and a variety of skin disorders (Stein and Shamoian 1981). More recently there has been a change in perspective on these and other disorders. Specific psychological causes are typically not sought, as there has been little success in identifying their relationship to particular disorders (there is still some controversy about this). Instead, researchers have begun to look at the interaction between life events or stresses, individual personality patterns, and the development of or susceptibility to disease. Rather than viewing certain diseases as psychologically based, investigators are now looking at the psychological factors that play a part in the disease process as a whole and trying to identify the salient variables for specific diseases. It has become clear that psychological and environmental factors can influence the onset and course of an illness, and medical diseases are now seen as multifactorially determined (Stein and Shamoian 1981). Certain factors may predispose people to illness, others may precipitate an illness episode, and others may sustain illness once an episode has occurred (Gottschalk 1978).

Stress linked to particular life events has been identified as an important factor in the development of a number of disorders. Holmes and Rahe (1967), among others, have developed a scale that rates a number of common life events in terms of the degree of stress associated with each event. A series of studies looked at stress levels and their relationship to the onset of illness (reviewed in Minter and Kimball 1980). An attempt was made to identify which individuals are at risk for the development of an illness, but not to determine what type of illness would occur. These studies often showed a relationship between stress levels and illness onset; however, methodological problems have somewhat attenuated these findings, and further research is needed before broad conclusions can be drawn. Friedman and Rosenman (1978) studied the relationship of personality variables to coronary artery disease. They described what they call Type A and Type B personalities; these types are thought to have a correlation to the incidence of coronary artery disease in men. The Type A individual is characterized as intense and hard-driving, and factors such as hostility, depressiveness, ambition, sociality, work activities, and strivings for independence have been identified as associated with the Type A personality and with ischemic heart disease. There is growing evidence that factors such as these play a role in disease development, but the nature of that role is still not clear. However, the importance of this work cannot be overlooked from a health care perspective: It has become clear that illness is not a unitary phenomenon tied exclusively to physiological processes. Illness can be associated in a variety of complex ways with psychological and environmental factors that must be understood if comprehensive and adequate treatment is to be carried out. This requires that we understand the issues that individuals routinely face throughout their lives, which people these issues became stressors for, and when life events do not follow a typical pattern, resulting in stress.

SUMMARY AND CONCLUSIONS

Middle adulthood is ushered in by a period of reexamination and questioning of former goals, values, and achievements and a change in time orientation related to facing one's own mortality. There is evidence that this period can be a crisis for many people; but others make the transition from young to middle adulthood quite smoothly. The self-examination initiated during the early part of this life phase can have a variety of effects on both work and family life. Its results can range from acute disruption to renewed commitments. Families must deal with the loss of children, the gaining of extended-family members through marriage, grandparenthood, and death, while trying to maintain a sense of integrity and cohesiveness that is often difficult to achieve. Work can be a source of great satisfaction for those who have reached appropriate levels of advancement; but it may be a source of profound disappointment for those who have plateaued at a lower level of advancement than they feel capable of. During this period, the consequences of earlier life-styles begin to be felt in the types of health problems that arise. There is an increasing incidence of depression, heart disease, stroke, and cancer, coupled with broader physiological changes of which individuals become aware. Changes in life patterns and in the culture may slowly affect the incidence of these diseases and the nature of the adjustment during this period.

4

HEALTH AND AGING

Older adults have been a relatively neglected group in the field of developmental psychology; only in the 1970s did interest surge in this phase of the life cycle. The same has been true in the health care fields. For example, a recent report stated that "with few exceptions, education in aging is deficient at all levels of medical education" (Institute of Medicine 1978, p. 45) and went on to note that interest in such education among medical students seems to be increasing and that there is a growing awareness of the problem.

Although there is much overlap of terms in usage, "gerontology" usually refers to the general study of aging and "geriatrics" denotes clinical or medical aspects of aging. This distinction is illustrated by the decision of the American Nurses Association in 1976 to change the name of their national practice division, Geriatric Nursing, to Gerontological Nursing Practice (Wells 1979), thus implying that nurses should deal with the process of aging and with the individual's functional state in addition to the medical diagnosis or disease (Stone 1980). Another definition that must be made is the age at which a person becomes elderly. The time of life termed "aging" conventionally begins at age 65, a demarcation point selected by Bismarck in the 1880s for legislation concerning retirement pensions. However, there are numerous criteria that can be used to determine when a person joins the ranks of the elderly, and each could justify a different dividing line. Due to developments such as the lengthening of the life span, improved health care, and the change in mandatory retirement age from 65 to 70, the beginning of "old age" in the public mind may well be pushed back. Already a noted gerontologist has proposed that persons beween the ages of 55 and 75 be known as the young-old and those over 75 as the old-old in order to more accurately reflect differences in probable level of functioning (Neugarten 1975). Although many studies, especially less recent ones, lump all elderly persons together, it should be remembered that individual differences increase with chronological age and that the elderly population segment is the least homogeneous (Kelly 1955). In this text the chapters on later adulthood will refer to individuals aged 65 and over in

FIGURE 4.1. Percentage of the American population 65 and older from 1900 to 1975, with predictions for 1980 to 2030.

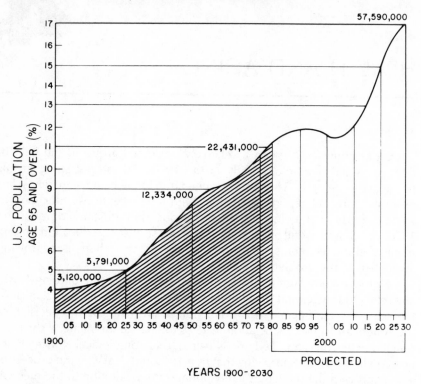

Source: R. N. Butler, "Introduction," in *Second Conference on the Epidemiology of Aging,* edited by S. Haynes and M. Feinleib, NIH Publication No. 80-969 (Washington, D.C.: U.S. Department of Health and Human Services, Public Health Service, 1980), p. 3.

order to conform to the definition used by most researchers. Distinctions between different groups will be made when data permit. The following sections provide a frame of reference. The elderly, even more than younger adults, need to be considered in the social, cultural, and biological contexts if their psychological development is to be understood.

DESCRIPTION OF THE ELDERLY POPULATION

Persons aged 65 and above made up only 4% of the U.S. population in 1900, but by 1980 that figure had jumped to 11% (see Figure 4.1). Assuming a moderate fertility rate of 2.1 births per woman, by the year 2030 18.3% of the population will be elderly (Treas 1981). If mortality rates

remain constant, three-quarters of those born in the U.S. in 1975 will survive to age 64, one-half to age 75, and one-quarter to age 85. Older adults,
therefore, are a major segment of the population, a segment that in 1977
included 23 million individuals (Kovar 1977).

Within this older group, 60% are female. The deficit of males increases
sharply with advancing age, from 80 males per 100 females in the 65-to-69-
year range to only 47 per 100 among those 85 years and over. The main
reason for this change is that male mortality has been higher than female
mortality at each age of life for many decades in the United States (Siegel
1980). Interestingly, even in the USSR, where men and women occupy
more equal occupational roles than in the United States, there is a 10-year
difference in life expectancy. The difference appears to be due to a combination of social, genetic, and biological factors.

Among white Americans, 11% are over age 65; the figure is only 7.4%
for blacks and 4% for the Spanish-surnamed population (Siegel 1980).
However, for those who live to age 70 the life expectancy for all groups is
about the same, perhaps indicating a survival of the fittest among the
disadvantaged minorities. The concept of multiple jeopardy, or additive
disadvantages (that is, the disadvantages of age are added to the disadvantages already experienced by minorities), is an important one for the
study of minority aged (Bengtson, Kasschau, and Ragan 1977).

At any given time, only 4 to 5% of persons over age 65 are living in a
nursing home or other institution. However, surveys reveal that 20% will
spend time in a nursing home before death, and of those over 80, almost
half will die in a nursing home (Butler 1978). Most older persons live in
family settings; about one-quarter live alone or with nonrelatives. Especially among older women, a trend has been noted toward living independently rather than with children or other relatives (Carp 1976). This
trend is not an indication that adult children no longer wish to care for
aging parents; rather, it reflects the well-established finding that older
parents usually express strong preference for remaining independent of
their children. Both older adults and their children maintain high levels of
contact and helping, even when they live far apart (Alpert and Richardson
1980).

Economically, the aged population is poorer than any other age segment. Although older couples have standards of living similar to those of
younger families, most elderly who do not live in families are living in or
bordering on poverty (Atchley 1980). Older women and members of racial
and ethnic minorities are most likely to find themselves impoverished,
often for the first time in their lives. Because most older people are dependent upon a fixed income, they are especially hard hit by inflation and unpredictable expenses such as hospitalization. This low income produces
dangerous deficiencies in level of living, particularly in areas such as food

and medical care. For example, the lack of adequate nutrition of many elderly is a significant contributing factor in disease and can lead to symptoms of "senility," with resulting premature institutionalization. Medical services remain a major expense for older adults and therefore may be used only when medical conditions have become serious. Although Medicare, a program of health insurance administered by the Social Security Administration, covers almost all persons over age 65, it pays only about half of medical expenses. The remaining amount must come from personal savings, private insurance, and other sources (Aiken 1978).

Despite the economic burden of medical expenses, older persons' use of health resources is significantly higher than that of other adults. Although they make up only 11% of the population, the personal health care expenditures of the aged account for 30% of the total for all Americans. The increased use of health care resources is especially pronounced among those aged 85 and over. Elderly individuals take one-quarter of all medications and fill one-third of all acute hospital beds in this country. More than 90% of the beds in chronic-care facilities are used by the aged. As one might expect, older adults account for as many as one-third of the patients seen by general physicians and an even larger proportion of those seen by internists (Blanchette 1980).

ATTITUDES TOWARD OLDER ADULTS

It is widely accepted in the field of gerontology that the elderly are the objects of strongly rejecting attitudes. Recent surveys have found that this is not the case: Lutsky (1980), in a review of the literature to date, concluded that "the absence of a strong negative stereotype of elderly persons and old age was noted" (p. 327). However, he also found that, although attitudinal evaluations are usually neutral or positive, they are lower than those for other age groups and they are variable, ranging from moderately positive to moderately negative, depending partially on the characteristics of the rater. For example, professionals who work with older adults in some capacity tend to rate them in a neutral or positive manner, while preprofessional students exhibit less positive attitudes. Furthermore, in several different studies, students in fields such as social work, law, medicine, and dentistry indicated that they preferred to work with younger adults and that few would even consider specializing in work with elderly people (Lutsky 1980).

The data regarding change of attitudes during professional training are mixed; some studies report deteriorating evaluations of the aged over the course of training and others find no change (Holtzman, Beck, and Ettinger 1981). It has been hypothesized that lack of training and knowledge contributes to health professionals' relatively low interest in and evaluation of the elderly. For example, Holtzman, Beck, and Ettinger found that positive attitudes and accurate knowledge were positively correlated. In a survey of practicing dentists, physicians, and registered nurses (Anderson and Burdman 1981), it was found that only 20% of dentists and physicians had received any training in geriatrics as compared to 50% of nurses. Physicians were the least interested in taking continuing education courses in geriatrics, while nurses were most interested. All groups "felt most comfortable" working with adults in the 20-to-49-year age range, not surprising when one remembers that many reported no training whatsoever in geriatrics.

It was noted earlier that researchers have not found that the general public holds strongly negative attitudes toward the elderly. Attitudes, which are evaluative, must be differentiated from beliefs, which concern knowledge. A major investigation of public beliefs concerning old age and older persons was conducted by Louis Harris and Associates for the National Council on Aging (Harris and Associates 1975). Results of this survey revealed that a fair amount of accurate information is held overall, with several specific areas of misconception. Americans tend to overestimate the amount of time the elderly spend watching television, sleeping, and engaging in other passive activities. Relative to older persons' self-reports, beliefs also overemphasized the seriousness of a number of problems experienced by the elderly. Other studies have found that Americans consistently overestimate the percentage of old persons in the population, the percentage in long-term care institutions, the extent of official poverty among the aged, the amount of boredom older people experience, and changes in religiosity with age (Lutsky 1980).

TRAINING IN GERONTOLOGY AND GERIATRICS

Unfortunately, past disregard for the study of aging was so pervasive that even today only a minority of training programs for health professionals require courses in gerontology or geriatrics. A number of reasons for past and current neglect of the elderly in health care fields have been posited. Many of these reasons concern negative attitudes and misconceptions. Sherman (1979) used the term "medical agism" to describe a type of prejudice against the elderly manifested by a distinct avoidance of older patients by physicians and surmised that much of this is learned in training: " 'Crock,' 'gomer,' and 'turkey' are terms that most physicians who have spent time in emergency rooms and acute wards have heard from the mouths of professional colleagues referring to elderly patients with strokes, dehydration, congestive heart failure, or cancer" (p. 3). A common misconception among health professionals has to do with their pessimism about the efficacy of treatment with the aged. Many symptoms are passed off as inevitable accompaniments of old age. In reality, sick old people are sick because they are sick, not because they are old. Among geriatricians a popular story has an 85-year-old woman going to her doctor and complaining of pain in her right leg. "What can you expect at your age?" says the doctor, to which the woman replies, "But my left leg is 85 too, and it feels fine!"

Sherman cited other common misconceptions that contribute to medical agism, including the idea that elderly people do not have interesting diseases and the notion that most older patients are like those found in nursing homes and acute-care hospitals. Newer training programs are attempting to introduce students to noninstitutionalized elderly people as well. Compounding the general problem of negative attitudes and beliefs is the fact that work with older persons may stimulate fears of aging, i.e., "they" will be "us." Furthermore, unresolved feelings toward parents may be brought to the forefront during contacts with the elderly.

PHYSICAL HEALTH AND AGING

Aging is a complex, multidimensional process that begins at conception. It may be divided into three major types: biological, psychological, and social. A bewildering array of definitions of biological aging exist, but fortunately most gerontologists have accepted a series of basic concepts concerning aging. These concepts have been summarized by McKenzie (1980, p. 28) as follows:

> (1) Aging is an extremely complex phenomenon. (2) There are many different types of aging. (3) Different rates of aging occur among different individuals. (4) Within each individual, different types of aging progress at different rates. (5) Aging is a universal characteristic of living organisms. (6) Genetic and environmental factors influence aging. (7) Aging entails change. (8) Aging is irreversible. (9) Aging progresses whether or not we can actually see it. (10) The exact cause or causes of aging are unknown.

Aging is not a disease and, contrary to popular belief, people do not die of old age. Therefore, it is especially important to be able to differentiate between normal and pathological aging. The normal physical changes in later adulthood have been summarized by Weg (1978) and are presented in Table 4.1. It should be noted that "normal" is used in the statistical sense and refers to changes currently seen in a majority of elderly individuals. Aging is extremely variable among human beings, and an 80-year-old may have a total physiological capacity equal to that of the average person 10 or 20 years younger. Furthermore, organ systems within the individual age at different rates so that a 70-year-old woman may have the renal functioning of the average 60-year-old and the cardiac output of

TABLE 4.1. Physical Changes That Accompany Normal Aging

---

1. Cell death is a time-related phenomenon of probable influence and
significance in the physiological manifestations of aging.
    (a) The loss of cellular units by death in skin, blood, liver, gastro-
intestinal tract, and bone marrow is partially compensated through replacement.
However, the rate of destruction may exceed rate of replacement with increased
age.
    (b) The loss of cellular units in the central nervous system, muscle,
and kidney is representative of loss in the kinds of cells that no longer
have the power of cell division or regeneration. These may be most crucial
in the aging processes. In the nervous system, for example, the functional
neurons may be replaced but by nonfunctional glial cells. So we are talking
about death of units and decrease in function of those that remain.

2. There is good agreement that there are changes in fibrous proteins.
Elastin fibers become thicker and aggregate, and are less elastic. The
collagen fibers become less soluble. These changes in turn influence the
structure and composition of the skin, the vasculature, and those very
important joints.

3. There is good evidence for changes in mineral metabolism. Calcium, for
example, under dietary and hormonal changes, may leave the bone and invest
the soft tissues. It may enter into the lining of arterioles and into the
joint sacs, leading to narrowed blood vessels and pain. Stiffening the rib
joints, there may be increased difficulty in breathing. Changes in the bone
structure may cause reduction in height, the familiar stooped posture, and
limitations in mobility - all earmarks of advanced years.

4. There is a measurable, progressive reduction of basal oxygen consumption
by the aging person. This reflects the lowering of reserve in all body
functions. Since we can only do that for which energy is available, we
can't do as much as we get older. For example, necessary synthesis of the
stuff of protoplasm decreases. More biochemical studies would provide information to substantiate these changes of time, exercise, and disease. Research
could demonstrate the reduction in available oxygen and the use of O_2 even
when it is available. The more molecular information we can gather, the
closer we may come to a real understanding of basic aging processes.

5. There is evidence for measurable change in heart and blood vessel
structure and function. Blood vessels narrow to cause increased peripheral
resistance. Blood pressure increases with age, and can be modified by
environmental, genetic, and cultural factors. There is a decrease in the
capacity of the heart to respond to extra demands, to the stress of heavy
work, and to emotional tensions. Any sclerotic changes in the vessels of the
brain may contribute to identifiable psychological symptoms.

6. We know that breathing may be less efficient due to changes in the muscles
of the ribs and chest, arteriosclerotic changes in lung blood vessels, changes
in elastic fibers, and/or changes in rib joints. As a consequence, less
oxygen is available to reach all tissues of the body.

TABLE 4.1. (cont.) Physical Changes That Accompany Normal Aging

---

7. There is evidence for changes in the gastrointestinal tract. A number of frequently cited physical factors attest to this. There is a decrease in sense of smell and taste, a loss of teeth, problems with dentures, a reduced mobility of stomach and intestines, a reduced secretion of digestive juices, constipation, hemorrhoids, malnutrition, and a decrease in fluid intake. Unfortunately, there is an increase in desire for, and consumption of, sweets. Often this is in the role of fulfilling psychological needs, rather than essential hunger.

8. There is agreement that changes in the genito-urinary tract present the aging individual with new concerns and threats to his dignity and personality. There is an increase in urinary incontinence and in frequency of urination. With men, this is often related to the enlargement of the prostate. With women, this is often accompanied by infection of the urethra or the bladder. Atrophic changes of genital tissues in men and women are expected changes with time. Natural involutional changes accompany the decrease in gonadal secretions and lead to a gradual atrophy of vaginal tissues after menopause, a decrease in lubrication, and a decrease in the size of the uterus and cervix.

9. Some of the other endocrine glands also come in for gradual, measurable changes. There is a marked decrease in the ability to fight disease as well as an increase in autoimmune properties. This loss of recognition of self often leads to the destruction of one's own tissues.

10. There are notable changes in the nervous system, the chief coordinating integrating mechanism of the human body. Reaction time and speed of movement slow down. This effect is common to different sensory modalities and several different motor pathways. Simple neurological function which involves few connections in the spinal cord remains virtually unchanged. It is the complex connections of the central nervous system that aging appears to affect mostly, contributing to memory loss, to difficulties with decision making, and to the decrease in homeostatic capacity. In any parameter we choose to monitor – heart rate, blood pressure, resistance to infection – the management of the displacement is greater and the rate of recovery is slower.

11. And finally we find empirically that there is an increased susceptibility to disease, particularly chronic disease. There appears to be a statistically significant increase in death from causes that earlier would not have had that result.

Source: Weg, R. "Physiological Changes That Influence Patient Care."
In Psychosocial Needs of the Aged: A Health Care Perspective,
edited by E. Seymour. Los Angeles: The Ethel Percy Andrus
Gerontology Center, University of Southern California, 1978,
pp. 9-12.

the average person several years older. Because of this variability, chronological age (or age in years) is not necessarily an indicator of biological or psychological age. In fact, as more has been learned about the aging process, it has become increasingly clear that knowing a person's chronological age is in many ways less useful than having an indication of his or her functional age (or ability to operate efficiently and effectively).

Theories of Biological Aging

Perhaps because of the complexity of the aging process, there are at least ten different theories to explain biological aging. Most are based on one particular aspect of the aging process. Although there is as yet no one theory that adequately accounts for all the changes with age that have been observed, the weight of evidence suggests that "the aging process represents a cumulative, age-related summation of the inherited program for aging, combined with the effect of accumulating environmental insults suffered by an individual from infancy through old age" (Rockstein and Sussman 1979, p. 37).

One of the most commonsensical of the better-known theories is the *wear and tear theory,* which is based on the notion that, through use, various parts of the body simply wear out. This hypothesis involves the concept of programmed aging and is supported by the fact that muscle fibers and nerve cells are unable to replace themselves when destroyed by wear and tear or by specific injury.

The *autoimmune theory* hypothesizes that bodily systems begin to reject their own tissues. That is, the body's immune system, with age, loses the ability to differentiate "self" from foreign material. Autoimmune reactions have been found in cardiovascular diseases, cancer, and diabetes, all major causes of death in the elderly.

The *metabolic waste theory* suggests that with age, harmful waste products of cellular metabolism accumulate in the cells of a number of organs, including the heart and the brain. One of the more notable of these waste products is lipofuscin, a pigment that is hypothesized to interfere with cell functioning by a displacement of other components within the cell. It is not clear, however, whether this buildup of waste products is a cause or a result of the aging process.

The *mutation theory* of aging is based upon the observation that a higher incidence of chromosomal aberrations is found in older than in younger animals. These aberrant cells, or mutants, are thought to be due to faulty genetic transmissions to dividing cells. Followers of this theory propose that changes associated with aging are caused by an accumulation of these mutations, which may ultimately lead to death.

The final biological theory of aging we will discuss is termed the cross-link or collagen theory. Many important molecules over time develop bonds between component parts of the same molecule or between different molecules. These cross-links alter the properties of the molecules involved so that they are unable to function as they did before. Much of the research in this area has been carried out with collagen, a fibrous protein that constitutes about one-quarter of total body protein. Results of promising research with animal subjects suggest that the formation of these cross-links can be slowed and that, once formed, they may be broken.

Physical Health of the Elderly

Researchers have compiled an impressive body of evidence that indicates that there are significant differences between young and elderly adults in their reaction to illness. As Hickey (1980) pointed out, these differences are of three types: physical/physiological, organismic/systemic, and mental/emotional. Physical and physiological changes with age are especially important in their effect on the individual's perception of and reaction to pain. Because of this, medical conditions may occur with symptoms different from those seen in younger persons. Pain may be nearly absent in acute appendicitis, for example, or myocardial infarction. The same may be true for an elderly individual's body temperature, which may rise only slightly even with the presence of significant infection (Hickey 1980). Changes in the organismic/systemic sphere reduce the individual's ability to withstand physical stress. As a result, the individual is less able to respond effectively to a sudden acute problem or to a prolonged and draining chronic condition. Mental and emotional components are important in determining an elderly person's response to illness because of the often extended length of treatment and combinations of problems. Older people frequently worry that sickness may lead to disability, dependency, or death. For others, an illness may force them to come to terms with their own advanced age.

Many people do not realize that at age 65, females have an average of 16.3 years of life remaining and males have 12.8 (Shanas and Maddox 1976). During this later phase of the life cycle, 50% of people surveyed report their health as good, 30% as fair, and 20% as poor. About two of every three persons report no trouble in carrying out activities of daily living, about one of every sixteen reports a great deal of trouble, and the remainder report some trouble (Shanas 1980). Thus, despite an increase in vulnerability to disease, there is no universal decline in health and physical ability after age 65. The elderly show great variability in patterns of change. For the majority, health remains fairly stable or fluctuates slightly when illnesses or accidents occur and recoveries are made. There is some evidence that much of the decline in abilities seen among older people is due more to lack of exercise and activity than to the aging process itself. This is especially likely before the mid-70s, at which time health concerns markedly increase.

Persons over age 65 actually have only half the incidence of acute illnesses that younger people suffer, but when elderly people are ill, they have more days of restricted activity (Institute of Medicine 1978). There is a higher prevalence of chronic conditions among the elderly than the young, about 81% as compared to 54%. However, these figures include minor conditions such as mild hearing loss and need for eyeglasses. When one looks at data on people with chronic conditions that limit activity it can be seen that the percentages both drop significantly. Therefore, although a significant increase in chronic conditions with age does indeed occur, there are surprisingly many elderly people who escape serious limitation. Among those with chronic health problems, women have higher rates than men for arthritis, diabetes, hypertension, back pain, and visual impairments. Men have higher rates of asthma, chronic bronchitis, hernia, peptic ulcer, and hearing impairment.

The prevalence of chronic conditions is one explanation for much of the inability of the current health care system to meet the needs of the elderly. The system in the United States has been set up to treat acute conditions in hospital settings, so many health care professionals are not interested in or become frustrated quickly with an individual whose chronic illness does not respond quickly to treatment. Furthermore, many older people need community-based care that is either not available or prohibitively expensive.

Causes of death among the elderly have been shifting toward chronic diseases and away from infectious-parasitic causes. Within the chronic diseases, patterns have also been changing, with an increasing incidence of deaths due to heart disease. Table 4.2 illustrates mortality rates for the ten leading causes of death among older adults in 1976. Cardiovascular disease, malignant neoplasms (cancer), and cerebrovascular disease (mainly strokes) together account for 70% of all deaths in persons over age 45; heart disease alone accounts for 40%. This pattern is found in most industrial societies (Shanas and Maddox 1976).

Health-Related Attitudes, Beliefs, and Behaviors

We noted earlier that an older person's psychological response to illness is often different from that of a younger person. Because these reactions are based on cultural and personal attitudes and beliefs, each is unique. More important, each influences both the medical services sought and the degree of disability experienced.

An example is provided by Shanas (1974), who, in a cross-national

TABLE 4.2.   Death Rates for the 10 Leading Causes of Death
              for Ages 65 and Over, by Age: 1976

(Deaths per 100,000 population)

Cause of death by rank	65 years and over	65 to 74 years	75 to 84 years	85 years and over
All causes	5,428.9	3,127.6	7,331.6	15,486.9
1. Diseases of the heart . . .	2,393.5	1,286.9	3,263.7	7,384.3
2. Malignant neoplasms	979.0	786.3	1,248.6	1,441.5
3. Cerebrovascular diseases .	694.6	280.1	1,014.0	2,586.8
4. Influenza and pneumonia . .	211.1	70.1	289.3	959.2
5. Arteriosclerosis	122.2	25.8	152.5	714.3
6. Diabetes mellitus	108.1	70.0	155.8	219.2
7. Accidents	104.5	62.2	134.5	306.7
Motor vehicle	25.2	21.7	32.3	26.0
All other	79.3	40.4	102.2	280.7
8. Bronchitis, emphysema and asthma	76.8	60.7	101.4	108.5
9. Cirrhosis of liver	36.5	42.6	29.3	18.0
10. Nephritis and nephrosis . .	25.0	15.2	34.1	64.6
All other causes	677.5	427.8	908.6	1,683.8

Source: Siegel, J. S. "Recent and Prospective Demographic Trends for the
         Elderly Population and Some Implications for Health Care". In
         Second Conference on the Epidemiology of Aging edited by S. Haynes
         and M. Feinleib, NIH Publication No. 80-969. Washington, D.C.:
         U.S. Department of Health and Human Services, Public Health
         Service, 1980, p. 305.

study of health behavior among the elderly, divided national groups into
health pessimists (Eastern Europe and Near East) and health optimists
(Western Europe and United States), based on self-rated health. More than
half the elderly British felt their health was good, as did Americans.
However, while the British were optimistic apparently to avoid complaining and making trouble, older Americans' optimism seemed based on "an
American self-image of activity and wellness in which any admission of

illness is a sign of weakness" (p. 613). It is likely that this American in-
tolerance of physical limitation and dependency hampers elderly people's
ability to gracefully accept unavoidable disabilities when they do occur. By
contrast, British elderly people have lower expectations for health in old
age and therefore are less concerned about limitations (Hickey 1980).
Another factor that makes it difficult for older Americans to adjust to
chronic disease is the emphasis of this country's health care system on
acute care and cure, as mentioned earlier. Regarding this, Hickey (1980,
p. 95) has written that

> Responses from health-care providers are confusing for their lack of appropriate
> attention, since medical help is focused primarily on curing disease rather than
> on providing adaptive or comfort measures for the chronically ill. This kind of
> response is especially disconcerting to most chronically ill individuals because
> they expect to be cured, and the belief in the prospect of recovering or, at least,
> getting better is usually a dimension of most individuals' psychological context
> of health.

Despite these difficulties, the elderly are no more likely than young
adults to inflate medical symptoms and ask for unnecessary medical treatment. In fact, the opposite is true: Underreporting symptoms is more common among the elderly than overreporting (Shanas 1976). Most older
persons either stoically underreact to serious symptoms or believe that
symptoms are due to old age and so are untreatable. Only a small proportion of elderly fall into the category with which most health care professionals are most familiar: those who have excessive bodily concern and
who are preoccupied with even minimal changes in functioning. These
persons are especially difficult to treat, and their "repetitive complaints,
relative to a variety of functional impairments, may result in over-testing,
overtreatment, and an unsatisfactory relationship between doctor and patient unless these complaints are seen as part of the patient's reaction to a
variety of physical, psychologic, and social changes" (Institute of Medicine
1978, p. 13).

Many reasons have been put forward to explain the reluctance to seek
treatment of the majority of the elderly, who are more likely to seek
medical attention only late in the development of disease. It is not that they
are poor assessors of their own health and illness. Rather, they tend to
believe that a doctor cannot help them or that they are not sick enough to
"bother the doctor." Nuttbrock and Kosberg (1980) found that older people's commonly held belief that "physicians do not really care about them
and are not interested in them" was associated with underutilization of
health services. Another contributing factor in this country is the equating
of illness or incapacity with weakness, as mentioned above (Shanas 1976).
Finally, Haug (1981) found that those elderly people who were more

TABLE 4.3.   Physician Visits (Nonhospital Settings) of Persons
Age 65 and Over by Reported Diagnosis

Rank	Diagnosed Disease/Problem	Percent of Total
1	Nervous system, sensory impairments	10.4
2	Circulatory system	9.2
3	Essential hypertension	8.8
4	Chronic ischemia	8.5
5	Arthritis and rheumatism	6.7
6	Chronic respiratory problems	5.9
7	Aftercare to hospitalization	5.9
8	Chronic genitourinary problems	4.7
9	Accidents	4.5
10	Neoplasms	4.0
11	Diabetes mellitus	3.9
12	Skin problems	3.5
	All others	24.0

Source: USDHEW National Center for Health Statistics.
National Ambulatory Medical Care Survey:
1973 Summary.   Publication No. 76-1772, 13(21).
Washington, D.C.:   Public Health Service, 1975.

knowledgeable about health were more likely to seek medical attention at
the appropriate time.

The diagnoses of those elderly people who visit a physician at his or
her office are presented in Table 4.3. These data demonstrate the prevalence of chronic disorders among this age group and support the finding
that only a minority of visits are for trivial complaints. Regarding actual frequency of physician visits among different age groups, Table 4.4 indicates
that the number of visits correlates significantly with the degree of

TABLE 4.4. Number of Physician Visits per Adult per Year, by Chronic Activity Limitation Status, Sex, and Age: United States, 1974

Sex and Age	Total Population	With No Limitation of Activity	With Limitation of Activity			
			Total	Limited But Not in Major Activity*	Limited in Amount or Kind of Major Activity	Unable to Carry On Major Activity*
	Number of Physician Visits per Person per Year					
Both Sexes						
17-44 years	4.8	4.2	10.6	7.0	12.2	15.2
45-64 years	5.5	4.0	10.1	7.4	10.3	12.4
65 years and over	6.7	4.6	9.3	6.5	8.8	11.0
Male						
17-44 years	3.4	2.9	8.0	5.4	9.0	12.1
45-64 years	4.9	3.5	8.8	6.5	8.2	10.9
65 years and over	6.7	4.5	8.9	6.7	7.1	10.1
Female						
17-44 years	6.1	5.4	13.3	9.0	14.5	21.5
45-64 years	6.1	4.5	11.5	8.2	11.6	18.2
65 years and over	6.8	4.7	9.6	6.4	9.4	13.3

*Major activity refers to the ability to work, keep house, or engage in school or preschool activity.

Source: USDHEW National Center for Health Statistics. Health Characteristics of Persons with Chronic Activity Limitation: United States, 1974. Publication No. 77-1539, 10(112). Washington, D.C.: Public Health Service, 1976, p. 14.

limitation of activity experienced. It can be seen that, with no limitation of activity, the average numbers of visits for younger and older adults are 4.2 and 4.6, respectively. For men, there is a slight increase in number of visits with age, while for women the number is stable, excluding visits related to childbearing. The results of a recent longitudinal study on utilization of health services by Canadians support these conclusions (Mossey, Havens, Roos, and Shapiro 1981). The study found that, relative to other age groups, the "elderly are not, as has often been assumed, high consumers of ambulatory physician visits and hospital days. Rather, a very small proportion of elderly account for a very large share of service use, and a person's utilization behaviors appear to remain consistent over time" (p. 557).

MENTAL HEALTH AND AGING

It is difficult to estimate the prevalence rates of mental illness because of differing methods of and criteria for psychiatric diagnoses. However, combining data from several studies allows for the identification of range estimates and trends. Using this approach, Blazer (1980) reviewed the results of a number of prevalence studies with older adults and concluded that, among people living in the community, (1) 50 to 80% are not impaired by psychiatric disorder, (2) 10 to 40% show mild to moderate impairment, and (3) 5 to 10% exhibit significant or severe psychiatric impairment. Along similar lines, Kramer, Taube, and Redick (1973) summarized the results of several mental health surveys and estimated that no less than 2% and perhaps as many as 20% of the elderly are in need of mental health services.

An obvious question concerns rates of mental illness in younger versus older adults. Thus far, it is not clear whether older adults have more psychiatric disorders than other age groups. Blazer (1980, p. 257) stated the following:

> In many studies, the prevalence of neurosis declines with age. Four studies, however, show the rate of overall psychiatric impairment to be increased with age. Two studies show a general ascending order of psychiatric impairment with advancing age among women but not among men. It appears that the prevalence of schizophrenia declines with age but the prevalence of psychosomatic complaints and especially organic brain syndrome increases with age. The overall findings are therefore equivocal.

Just as it is useful and realistic to divide persons over age 65 into different age groups for other research purposes, it helps to look at the mental health of the young-old and the old-old. Among this latter group of people aged 75 and over, the probability of organic brain disorder increases considerably, while the rate of schizophrenia and other conditions declines.

Studies of the relationship between gender, age, and mental illness reveal an interesting reversal: Rate of psychosis for females aged 54 and under is higher than for males, but among people aged 55 and over the rate is lower for females (Blazer 1980). Data on prevalence of psychiatric impairment among older people of different races and ethnic origins are sparse (e.g., Jackson 1979). The relationship between social class and mental illness among the elderly is also largely unknown.

Epidemiological studies of psychiatric disorders in later life have identified several factors that are considered to be of etiologic significance. In addition to genetic and biochemical abnormalities, Blazer (1980) listed five psychosocial factors: stress, loss of social supports, maladaptive personality style, previous history of mental illness, and physical illness. As with the theories of biological aging discussed earlier, each of these factors has been studied in isolation, and a comprehensive model of causation remains to be developed.

Although older individuals may not be especially vulnerable to psychiatric impairment, a substantial number need mental health services. Unfortunately, the elderly receive fewer of these services than any other age group except young children. In 1973 people aged 65 and over constituted 2% of clients at outpatient clinics and 4% of clients at community mental health centers (Kramer, Taube, and Redick 1973). They are much more likely to be found in county and state hospitals than younger adults. Recently, nursing homes have become repositories for mentally impaired older people, a shift described as a step backward by Zarit (1980) and as an exclusion of the elderly from recent advances in treatment by Kahn (1975). Several reasons for this state of affairs are suggested by Zarit (1980), including negative attitudes toward the elderly, beliefs that they cannot be helped and will not benefit from treatment, a lack of professionals trained to work with older adults, and the reluctance of the elderly themselves to seek help for personal problems.

In the sections that follow we will review several of the more common psychiatric disorders found in old age. All categories of psychological disturbances covered here, except for the brain disorders, are classified as "functional disorders," which traditionally have been thought to occur in the absence of brain dysfunction. When brain function is thought to be impaired the resulting disorders are termed "organic." The disorders discussed here range from the mild and nondisabling to the severe and totally disrupting. It should be emphasized that these disturbances do not reflect normal changes with age.

Depression and Suicide

Depression is the most common functional psychological disorder among the elderly, accounting for one-quarter to one-half of all hospital admissions for this age group (Zarit 1980). It is also the most common complaint among older community residents, with an estimated 2 to 10% judged sufficiently depressed to receive a clinical diagnosis (Gurland 1976). It is not difficult to understand the reasons for this when we consider the multiple losses and changes that many people have to endure during their later years. Zung (1980, p. 353) asserted that "If we accept the criteria for health and normality as a person's ability to work and produce, to love and play, and to enjoy life, then we can see that the realities of life do not provide this for the elderly. Instead, real life events take place that impair the ability of the elderly to be normal."

The symptoms of depression among older adults most often involve anxiety, preoccupation with physical symptoms, withdrawal, apathy, and lack of drive. This pattern is considered different from that typically found in younger depressives, in whom feelings of sadness are reported more and somatic complaints and apathy, less often. The biggest difference probably lies in the importance of somatic complaints among elderly depressives; they may be the predominant or even the only reported problem. These people usually deny sad feelings, and the frequent comment one hears is, "I feel perfectly fine except for this backache (headache, etc.)." It is difficult to differentiate depression from normal mood changes and grief following losses, both of which may lead to symptoms of depression, such as sadness and withdrawal. Another important distinction is that between depression and dementia; an elderly individual may appear "demented" and even be institutionalized as a hopeless case when the root of the problem is a treatable depression. More will be said about this shortly in the section on organic mental disorders.

Although the elderly are usually excluded from research on psychotherapy for depression (Weissman and Myers 1979), clinical reports confirm the ability of depressed older adults to benefit from psychotherapy and/or drug therapy (e.g., Mintz, Steuer, and Jarvik 1981). Whatever approach is chosen, treatment of depression is especially important among older people because of the relatively high proportion of the depressed elderly who commit suicide. Physical illness is another important factor that increases the probability of suicide in old age. It is estimated that 25% of all suicides in the United States are committed by people over age 65, and even this figure is thought to be an underestimate, considering the many fatal "accidents" among the elderly. Figure 4.2 illustrates the pattern of suicide across the life cycle for nonwhite and white women and men. After age 25, the suicide rate increases with age for white men only and jumps dramatically after age 75. More recent data show essentially the same pattern (Botwinick 1978).

Other data on suicide among the elderly reveal that, whereas younger adults have a high proportion of unsuccessful attempts, older adults virtually always succeed in killing themselves. Most suicides in old age are

FIGURE 4.2. Suicide rates in the United States during 1964 in relation to age.

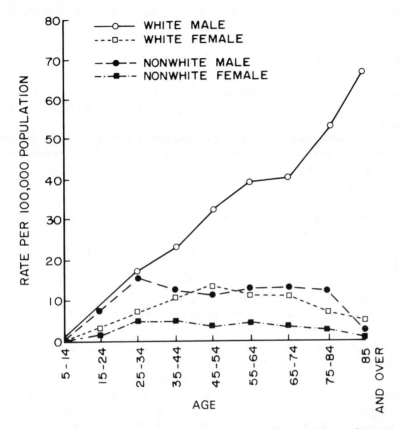

Source: U.S. Department of Health, Education, and Welfare, National Center for Health Statistics, *Vital and Health Statistics* 20(5) (Washington, D.C.: Public Health Service, 1967), p. 5.

preceded by depression (McKenzie 1980), and often signals are given to others that are not "read," such as giving away valued possessions and saying good-bye to family and friends. These indirect signals are more common among older people than the obvious threats and other signs often expressed by younger potential suicides.

Paranoid States

Paranoid states are the second most common functional psychological disorder found in older adults. They are characterized by the presence of a delusion or delusional system. Delusions are thoughts or beliefs that are false or contrary to reality. Paranoid symptoms can range from mild suspiciousness to firm belief in an elaborate delusional system, often involving persecution. These symptoms are hard to ignore and often are very disturbing to family and friends. One of the worst effects of paranoid symptoms is that they may drive away people who were valuable social supports. The paranoid individual may then find himself or herself increasingly isolated, a situation that is conducive to increased paranoia. This vicious circle may eventually lead to unnecessary institutionalization, an outcome that probably could have been avoided with proper treatment of the initial symptoms.

Zarit (1980) has identified four etiological factors that appear to contribute to paranoid disorders in later life. First, paranoid symptoms may be the extension of a chronic psychosis that began in earlier adulthood. Second, paranoid behaviors may appear as the result of a brain disorder, including those disorders precipitated by medication. Third, social isolation, as mentioned above, increases the probability of paranoid thinking. Finally, sensory losses, especially hearing loss, may lead to such symptoms. It has been hypothesized that elderly tend to "fill in" the gaps caused by sensory loss with their own unique material. For example, a woman who sees two people talking and looking in her direction, but who cannot hear them, may assume they are whispering about her.

It should be noted that some apparently paranoid symptoms may be based on reality. The elderly individual may be correctly perceiving various types of age discrimination, or agism, for example, "that physicians are less likely to give them careful examination and treatment, that bank officials are reluctant to give them loans, that landlords would like to evict them in order to raise the rent, that children would like to spend less time with them, that nursing home staff or other patients are removing possessions, and that they are less likely to be employed" (Eisdorfer 1980, p. 332).

Several treatment approaches for the elderly with paranoid symptoms have been developed, and although there is little experimental evidence, it appears that many patients respond favorably to one approach or a combination of approaches. These treatments include identification of sensory losses and restoration of function, provision of a supportive relationship, and medication. Changing the environment to reduce rewards for paranoid behavior and enhancing the individual's sense of control over his or her own life also are often helpful.

Hypochondriasis

Another relatively common disorder among the elderly is hypochondriasis, an excessive preoccupation with one's health or bodily function. This disorder is also especially disturbing to others, largely because of the lack of effect that reassurance or explanations have on the individual's complaints. It is generally thought that this problem is more common among older adults, but there is little evidence as yet to support this notion. Because of the larger proportion of elderly who suffer from chronic ailments, it is even more difficult to distinguish actual from exaggerated complaints than with younger people.

Very little is known about the etiology of hypochondriasis. It has been suggested that chronic physical diseases force elderly people to focus more on the body and thus lead to increased vulnerability to maladaptive preoccupation. Most research has examined two variables of etiological significance. The first has to do with the different ways in which people learn to respond to stress; the second concerns the rewards that accrue to hypochondriacs as a result of their symptoms, for example, avoidance of responsibilities that arouse anxiety (Zarit 1980).

Data on effective treatments for the disorder are also sparse. Hypochondriacs are reputed to be among the most difficult patients to treat, with good reason. When told nothing is physically wrong, they tend to seek additional opinions until they find a physician who will treat them. They are often overtreated and misdiagnosed, and after it all, the underlying problem remains. Busse and Blazer (1980) have developed a set of guidelines to aid in treating these individuals that emphasizes listening to the patient, indicating the presence of a "serious" but not "critical" condition, prescribing certain mild remedies, and having the patient return for visits on a regular basis with the same physician.

Sleep Disorders

Older adults often report disturbances of sleep involving difficulty in falling asleep, frequent awakening during the night, increased dreaming, lighter sleeping, and awakening early in the morning and being unable to go back to sleep. Many people do not realize that changes in the sleep pattern normally occur in later adulthood. These changes include taking more time to fall asleep and a decrease in the time spent in two of the stages of sleep, deep sleep (stage 4) and REM (rapid eye movement) sleep, the stage during which most dreaming occurs. There is an increase in the number of awakenings during the night (e.g., Amin 1976). The total amount of time spent in sleep decreases, especially in advanced age, although more time may be spent in bed.

Sleep disorders are reported by an estimated 50% of older adults (Kahn and Fisher 1969). Some of these individuals are responding to the effects of age changes on sleep. Others, however, may be noting sleep problems that are manifestations of depression or anxiety. Pfeiffer (1976) stated unequivocally that "sleep disturbances are involved in all of the major psychiatric illnesses of old age" (p. 201). Additional known causes of sleep disorders among the elderly are adverse drug reactions and a number of acute and chronic physical illnesses. Sleeping medications themselves may exacerbate disturbances in sleep, and with older adults they can cause confusion (Busse and Blazer 1980). Poor sleep habits also contribute to sleep disorders and include using the bed for watching television, exercising just before bedtime, going to bed when not sleepy, and napping during the day.

Treatment of sleep disturbances varies according to the cause; therefore its success depends on accurate assessment of the problem. Some successful treatment programs have involved relaxation training, habit changes, psychotherapy, judicious use of medications (including withdrawal of some), reducing daily stress, exercising during the day, changing thoughts such as "I'll never get to sleep," and getting out of bed at the same time every morning.

Alcoholism

Although the proportion of heavy drinkers in the population decreases with age, alcoholism is a serious problem for many older people. Estimates of prevalence range from 2 to 10%, depending on the specific elderly population being examined (Schuckit and Pastor 1979). Rates are even higher among widowers, those living in disadvantaged areas, and those with physical illness. Regarding age of onset, elderly alcoholics include those who have a long history of alcohol abuse and those who began problem drinking relatively recently.

Depression and confusion are usually present in actively drinking alcoholics, but many will return to a normal state after a few days of abstinence (Schuckit and Pastor 1979). Others, however, turn to alcohol as an antidote to depression or anxiety. Perhaps this latter group accounted for the success of Zimberg's (1975) treatment program, which consisted of antidepressant medication and a supportive relationship. Taken as a whole, the evidence, although sparse, suggests that elderly alcoholics with late-onset drinking respond well to treatment (Zarit 1980).

Brain Disorders

Organic mental disorders are the most common psychiatric (including both functional and organic) disorders of later life. Results of surveys indicate that 4 to 6% of the elderly show signs of definite brain disorder, and this figure jumps to 20% of those over age 80 (Kay 1972). These figures, contrary to the popular stereotype, show that most older people do not become "senile," although the proportion of the elderly with organic mental disorders does increase with age.

The study of brain disorders in the elderly is complicated by confusing terminology. Historically these disorders have been divided into two types: (1) those that are termed delirium, acute brain syndrome, and reversible dementia, and (2) those that have been called chronic brain syndrome, organic brain syndrome, senile dementia, and Alzheimer's-type dementia. With increasing knowledge, it has become apparent that there are problems with distinguishing the types on the basis of either the acute-chronic or the reversible-irreversible continuum. Partially for this reason, the most recent edition of the *Diagnostic and Statistical Manual of Mental Disorders* of the American Psychiatric Association (1980) refers to acute brain syndrome as "delirium" and to chronic brain syndrome as "primary degenerative dementia," the terms we will use here.

Delirium is a descriptive term that does not imply etiology or prognosis. The characteristics of this disorder include a clouding of consciousness, attentional deficit, perceptual disturbances, fragmented thinking, disturbance of the sleep-wakefulness cycle, and either increased or decreased psychomotor activity (American Psychiatric Association 1980). Emotional disturbances are common, as is fluctuation of symptoms. Many causes of delirium have been identified; they consist mainly of systemic illnesses, neurologic disorders, metabolic disorders, toxic drug reactions, other types of stress, and social isolation. Treatment is based on treatment of the underlying disorder, and in the absence of complications, the individual is often left with little or no change in previous level of functioning (Raskind and Storrie 1980).

Unlike the diagnosis of delirium, the diagnosis of primary degenerative dementia does assume a specific etiology, generally Alzheimer's disease. This is the most common type of dementia. The hallmark of dementia is impairment of memory, although declines in intellectual function, judgment, orientation, and emotional stability are also frequently noted. Changes in the brain found in persons with primary degenerative dementia include increased neurofibrillary tangles, which interfere with normal cell functioning, and senile plaques, degenerated cell structures that accumulate at synapses between cells and seem to interfere with conductance of nerve impulses. The causes of these brain changes are not known (Zarit 1980).

Depression in the elderly can be mistaken for dementia, and special care must be taken to correctly differentiate these two disorders. Several reviews of the pertinent literature have led to the conclusion that dementia is overdiagnosed in this country (e.g., Kart 1981). Recent studies, such as that by Fox, Topel, and Huckman (1975), suggest that 10 to 30% of dementia patients have a potentially treatable underlying disorder. In addition to depression, drug toxicity is a common cause of this "pseudo-dementia" (Libow 1973).

The second major type of dementia is multi-infarct dementia, caused by vascular disease leading to a reduced blood flow to and within the brain or by hypertension. It accounts for an estimated 10 to 20% of all dementias (Hachinski, Lassen, and Marshall 1974). Once a positive diagnosis has been made, there is no reason to assume nothing more can be done; although treatment cannot reverse or even halt the brain changes that are occurring, the affected individual and the family can often be helped by treating secondary behavioral problems and by individual and family counseling (Raskind and Storrie 1980; Zarit 1980).

SUMMARY AND CONCLUSIONS

People aged 65 and over constitute 11% of the population but account for 30% of Americans' total health care expenditures. Attitudes toward the elderly tend to be neutral or positive, but not as positive as those toward other age groups. Health professionals report preferences for work with younger adults, and only a small minority specialize or wish to specialize in work with the elderly. A major cause of this lack of interest is medical agism in student training.

There are a number of theories of biological aging, each of which explains only one or a few of the normal changes associated with age. Although incidence of chronic disease increases with age, there is no universal decline in health and physical ability after age 65. When disease does occur, the elderly are less likely than younger adults to seek medical care.

The evidence concerning a possible increase in psychiatric disorders with age is equivocal. Depression is the most common functional psychiatric disorder among the elderly, followed by paranoid states and hypochondriasis. Sleep disorders are reported more often in old age; alcoholism is seen less often. Despite its decreased incidence, alcoholism is an important health problem that is often overlooked by health professionals. Brain disorders affect up to 20% of those over age 80 and may be classified along several dimensions. Some brain disorders are caused by somatic illnesses, depression, or medications and may be reversible.

COGNITIVE PROCESSES
IN LATER ADULTHOOD

The study of intellectual and mental processes in old age is a major part of the psychology of aging. Traditionally, these cognitive processes are divided into topics such as memory, learning, problem-solving, and so on. However, it should be remembered that these distinctions are largely conceptual and break down rapidly as one becomes better acquainted with the nature of the processes. For example, it is very difficult to test learning without also assessing memory, as learning involves acquisition of knowledge and memory involves storing and then retrieving it.

Significantly more attention is devoted to these particular processes in the elderly than in young and middle-aged adults. The reason for this difference is the greater rate of change investigators have found in later adulthood. The changes themselves are gradual and often begin in middle age or even as early as the 20s. They may be noticed by the individual only very late in life and may cause little or no functional loss. Those changes that are the hallmarks of advanced age are minor loss of memory function and slowing of motor performance.

SENSATION AND PERCEPTION

Sensation and perception are often discussed as though they were two separate processes, but, like learning and memory, they are so closely related that it is difficult to discuss them separately. Sensation may be defined as input from physical stimuli; perception refers to the interpretation of sensory information. Age-related declines in both sensation and perception have been documented.

Sensation

Vision is one of the major areas in which research on the relationship between age and the senses has been conducted. Most deficiencies in vision with age can be traced to physiological changes such as reduced pupil size, loss of lens transparency, and reduced lens elasticity (McKenzie 1980). Acuity, or the ability to see small objects clearly at a distance, is stable until age 40 or 50 and then declines markedly (Botwinick 1978). These changes can usually be overcome through the use of magnifying lenses and higher levels of illumination. With decreases in illumination below moderate levels, the acuity of an elderly person will suffer much more than that of a younger adult (March 1980).

Accommodation refers to the problems of focusing on close objects. Most people become farsighted, or presyopic, with age; that is, they do not see well things that are close. The loss of accommodation is very gradual and begins in childhood, accelerates between ages 40 and 55, and then levels off (Bruchner 1967). Eyeglasses can usually correct the problem to a level where it is not disabling.

Studies examining changes with age in ability to visually adapt to the dark have consistently found that the elderly cannot see as well in the dark as young adults can. These results have clear practical implications, such as the need for the elderly to exercise special care when driving at night and the usefulness of night lights. Mixed results have been reported concerning age-related differences in speed of adapting to the dark (Botwinick 1978).

In another area of vision research, it has been reported that the ability to distinguish certain colors, notably blues, blue-greens, and violets, falls off after age 70 and that after age 85 this decrement becomes extremely pronounced. Discrimination of reds, oranges, and yellows is relatively stable across the life cycle. Practical implications of these sensory changes abound; for example, Botwinick (1978) suggested that if a physician asks an elderly patient to take both blue and green pills, some feature other than color should be used as identification so that the patient can distinguish between them.

Hearing is another major area in which research has produced evidence of decline with age. This decline occurs gradually and may never be noticed. Also, men experience more auditory loss than women do. Although the existence of hearing loss in old age is well established, Botwinick (1978) reviewed data that indicate that this loss may be overestimated in the elderly due to their cautiousness, a trait that leads to their reporting sounds only when they are sure they hear them. Experiential factors must also be considered as contributors to hearing loss; it is well known that people who are exposed to noisier environments earlier in life will exhibit greater loss than those who lived in quieter settings.

Specific auditory losses with age involve frequency and pitch discrimination. Most of these losses are caused by neural alterations in the auditory system (Marsh 1980). There is a gradual loss of sensitivity to sounds, especially at the higher frequencies, starting at least as early as age 20. This means that, at higher frequencies, tones must be louder for the elderly to be able to hear them. The name for this loss is presbycusis. Similarly, pitch discrimination, especially at the higher frequencies, decreases with age. The greater loss at higher frequencies would be expected, as these tones are the ones heard less well. Most of the hearing losses that occur in later adulthood can be corrected. When speaking to someone with impaired hearing, it helps to speak with a lower voice pitch, to speak more slowly and loudly, and to enunciate clearly.

Taste thresholds of older adults have been investigated for a variety of substances. The evidence generally indicates a slight reduction in taste sensitivity with age, a finding more pronounced for men than for women (Cowart 1981). Several studies have found decrements in sensitivity to olfactory stimulation in old age (e.g., Schemper, Voss, and Cain 1981). We do not know when this loss begins. As with taste, men appear more vulnerable to loss of smell sensitivity. The paucity of evidence renders these results tentative, however, as do the effects, as yet unknown, of health on olfaction. Health is implicated as an important factor because it is known that, with age, olfactory ability becomes susceptible to loss as a result of illness. This loss may occur as a result of a serious cold or influenza, for example, and may be both pronounced and permanent (McKenzie 1980). The physiological cause for this is not known.

The relationship between pain and age has received surprisingly little attention. The sparse data that exist indicate no major shift in pain thresholds in normal older adults (Harkins and Warner 1980). Research has not shed light on the relationship between age and pain tolerance or sensitivity to pain associated with pathology. Clinically, it is known that elderly individuals may experience less pain than younger adults for some conditions, such as myocardial infarction (Hickey 1980). The study of pain is complicated by the multiple determinants of pain response, which include sensory, emotional, and evaluative factors (Melzack and Dennis 1978).

Perception

Perception, it will be remembered, refers to the processing or interpreting of information from the senses. In his review of perception and aging, Botwinick (1978) divided the literature into three parts, each based upon research conducted with a different type of stimulus: sequential integration, temporal integration, and spatial integration.

When information comes to the perceiver one part at a time, it is processed sequentially. A classic type of experiment requiring sequential integration involves stimulus fusion. The stimulus may be a flashing light or a sound click. The light or click is presented to the viewer at a controlled pace that accelerates until the subject perceives that the stimulus lights or clicks "fuse" into a steady light or into fewer clicks. This fusing point comes sooner for older than for younger adults, a difference that has been attributed to physiological changes in the central nervous system as well as to peripheral changes in the eye or ear. It is theorized that, as a result, it takes a stimulus longer to "clear" the nervous system. In other words, the stimulus persists longer than would be the case for a younger person. This stimulus-persistence theory has proved useful for explaining the results of stimulus-fusion studies and other paradigms investigating sequential integration. It has also been hypothesized that stimulus persistence contributes to the difficulty older people have in understanding rapid speech. If the trace of one word or sound persists while the next is being heard, processing may be disrupted.

In studies requiring temporal integration, nonsequential information is used as the stimulus. Botwinick (1978) included in this category studies using spirals, colors, and visual illusions as stimuli. In spiral studies, a revolving spiral is presented to the subject for a set length of time. When the rotation of the spiral stops, the subject perceives an aftereffect of the spiral revolving for a short time. Contrary to what would be predicted by stimulus-persistence theory, elderly people show an aftereffect of shorter duration than young subjects do after viewing the spiral for less than 1 minute. Interestingly, however, when exposure to the spiral stimulus is longer, older adults report, as predicted, a longer aftereffect than younger adults (Griew, Fellows, and Howes 1963). After considering these and other findings, Botwinick (1978) suggested the following explanation, which supports stimulus-persistence theory: "With increasing age, more difficulty is encountered in processing inputs, and it takes more time to do so. But once they are incorporated into the perceptual system of the older person, they persist longer and result in a variety of effects" (p. 172).

Spatial-integration studies involve stimuli that are difficult to perceive because their parts are spread out or disguised. It has been found that there is an age-related decline in the ability to perceive such stimuli, a decline that is not adequately explained by stimulus-persistence theory. Neither is the theory especially useful in understanding the results of another spatial-integration study, in which the stimuli were a series of thirteen drawings, the first of which was a cat and the last a dog. The drawings were gradually modified so that the cat became the dog over the course of the drawings. Elderly subjects took longer to shift from perceiving the cat to perceiving the dog than did young subjects (Korchin and Basowitz 1956). Results of this and similar studies have been seen as reflecting a relative inability of older adults to switch from one way of perceiving stimuli to another, or perceptual rigidity.

Summary

In summary, age-related declines have been documented in the senses of sight, hearing, taste, and smell, but not in pain. These conclusions are more tentative for taste, smell, and pain due to the lack of relevant data concerning these senses in the elderly. For most people, sensory losses can be corrected and are not disabling. Perceptual declines in later adulthood have been noted with various stimuli requiring sequential, temporal, and spatial integration. Stimulus-persistence theory has proved useful in explaining losses only in sequential and temporal integration abilities with age.

LEARNING

Learning has been defined by Botwinick (1967) as the acquisition of information or skills. It is an internal process that cannot be observed or measured directly. Learning therefore must be measured on the basis of observable features, or external behaviors, from which learning is inferred. For older people especially, this distinction between learning and performance is important; failure to differentiate between the two led to an overestimation of learning deficits among elderly people for many years (Botwinick 1978). Until about 1960, researchers had repeatedly found marked declines in learning ability with age. However, they failed to take into account the noncognitive variables that influence the learning task, such as anxiety and the speed at which the task must be carried out. Once these factors were recognized, it became clear that much of the so-called learning deficit in the elderly was in fact attributable to difficulty in expressing the learned information. Currently, it is accepted that learning performance declines in later adulthood, but it is not known if learning ability itself declines with age (Botwinick 1978).

We mentioned above that learning and memory may be seen as part of the same system. This is the information-processing view of cognitive functioning, in which learning is merely the first step in the process. Prior to the acceptance of this approach in the 1970s, the paradigm used by researchers was the stimulus-response or rote-learning view (Arenberg and Robertson-Tchabo 1977). Most of the studies within the area of learning were carried out when the stimulus-response orientation was generally held. The majority of these that examined adult age differences in learning ability used the verbal-learning paradigm, which involves words or nonsense syllables (e.g., XUJ, BN). One major type of verbal-learning paradigm is termed paired-associate learning. Here, the subject is asked to learn the relationships or associations beween pairs of verbal cues, such as tree/floor and DL/CB. The subject is first given the entire set of paired verbal cues to learn within a given amount of time, the inspection interval. Then the first of each verbal cue pair is presented alone, and the subject is asked to provide the correct response within a given time, the response interval.

The other major verbal-learning paradigm is serial learning, in which the subject is presented with a chain of items to learn during the inspection interval and then must repeat the chain during the response interval. It may be noted that both these stimulus-response paradigms assign a relatively passive role to the subject, who is essentially a responder. Within the information-processing framework, the subject is seen as organizing and integrating input in a much more active fashion (Botwinick 1978).

Researchers during the past 20 years have uncovered a number of noncognitive factors, as mentioned earlier, that have been found to contribute to the observed differences in performance on learning tasks between younger and older adults. These include education, other past experience, physical health, brain disorders, amount of recent practice, and social isolation (Baltes and Labouvie 1973), in addition to variables having to do with characteristics of the task itself.

Pacing

Pacing refers to variations in the amount of time provided for the learning task. Both the inspection interval and the response interval may be manipulated by the experimenter or by the subject (self-pacing). Overall, studies indicate that older adults benefit more from both longer inspection and response intervals than younger adults do. For example, Canestrari (1963), using a paired-associate learning task, gave young and old subjects three different stimulus-pacing schedules: 1.5 seconds, 3.0 seconds, and self-paced. It was found that elderly people performed worst in the fast-paced condition and best when they were able to pace themselves and that most of the benefit appeared related to the longer response intervals that the elderly gave themselves. Even in the self-pacing condition, however, elderly people did not perform as well as young adults. Errors made by the older subjects that decreased with self-pacing were more likely to be those of omission (no responses given) than of commission (incorrect response given). Although Canestrari's results and those of several other investigators seem to indicate that the performance deficit is paramount, Botwinick (1978) warned that it would be premature to assume that there is only a learning performance deficit. Results of most relevant studies, including Canestrari's, have demonstrated age decrements even in self-paced conditions, suggesting a learning ability deficit.

Arousal

There is a body of data that suggests that older people become inappropriately aroused, or anxious, in experimental situations. This arousal appears to contribute to their lower level of learning performance. In an early study, Powell, Eisdorfer, and Bogdonoff (1964), using serial-learning tasks, looked at free fatty acid (FFA) levels as indicators of arousal. From blood samples taken before, during, and after the learning task, they determined that FFA levels were higher in older than in younger subjects throughout the experiment. In a later study, Eisdorfer, Nowlin, and Wilkie (1970) manipulated the level of arousal in subjects in order to examine its effect on learning performance. One group of elderly men was administered the drug propranolol, which inhibits arousal but does not affect cognitive processes. Another group was given a placebo, or sugar pills. The experimenters found that the group that had received propranolol had lower FFA levels and performed at a higher level than the placebo control group. They concluded that many learning deficits among the elderly may be the result of higher arousal in experimental settings.

Although there does seem to be an important relationship between arousal and learning performance in later life, differences between younger and older adults are not clear, and the role of motivational factors in arousal and performance still needs to be clarified (Botwinick 1978). Furthermore, there is some evidence that higher blood pressure, another indicator of arousal, is associated with improved performance in elderly subjects (Powell, Buchanan, and Milligan, cited in McKenzie 1980). McKenzie surmised that "the general concept of arousal can be employed with equal force to explain either inferior or superior performance exhibited within the learning situation" (p. 79).

Caution

As an explanation for the age decrement in learning, the concept of arousal is related to that of caution. Eisdorfer (1968) hypothesized that increased arousal led to greater caution in the learning situation, which decreased task performance. This hypothesis was based on his observation of large numbers of omission errors by elderly subjects, the same pattern reported by Canestrari (1963) among others. Support for this notion is provided by Leech and Witte (1971), who successfully reduced omission errors and improved elderly subjects' performances by paying them for both correct and incorrect responses. However, although age differences in cautiousness may account for differences in omission errors, cautiousness does not fully explain the age decrement in learning performance. This conclusion was reached by Okun, Siegler, and George (1978) in their investigation of cautiousness and verbal-learning performance. Young and old adults were administered two measures of cautiousness and were given a serial-learning task. Results indicated that age differences in cautiousness did not account for elderly subjects' lower performance.

Task Meaningfulness

Task meaningfulness, like caution, may be seen as a variable that can be manipulated to increase older subjects' "motivation" to do well on a laboratory task. For example, Hulicka (1967) reported that 80% of her elderly subjects refused to exert themselves to learn paired associates involving a word and a nonsense syllable and that they found the task difficult. She then changed the task to utilize meaningful pairs of words and was successful in obtaining task performance from the subjects. Their level of performance still did not equal that of younger adults, however.

Changing paired associates to make them more meaningful or familiar generally involves increasing the associative strength of the words, for example, from dog/LE to dog/cat. This manipulation makes the task easier and therefore confounds the interpretation of results: Are the elderly doing better under conditions of greater task meaningfulness because they do better on easier tasks in general or because lack of meaningfulness specifically contributes to their performance deficit? To try to answer this question, Wittels (1972) devised paired-associate lists of approximately equal strength of association for young and old adults. Each list was constructed to be particularly familiar and meaningful for either young or old subjects. Results indicated that the elderly performed worse on all lists than young adults, thus suggesting that task meaningfulness is not a sufficient explanation for the age decrement in paired-associate learning.

Other Noncognitive Factors in Learning

A number of other noncognitive factors that enhance the learning performance of older adults have also been investigated. One of these is providing techniques for organizing the information to be learned. Another is teaching mediational techniques designed to help subjects associate elements of information, for example, having them form a "word-picture" to link paired associates. Supportive instructions and an accepting atmosphere also function as aids in the learning performance of the aged. The final performance modifier for the elderly we will mention here is the reduction of interference in the learning situation. Optimally, when several pieces of information are being learned, the first should be learned well before the second is undertaken.

Summary

In summary, the learning literature indicates that there is an age-related decrement in learning ability and that there are factors that can improve the performance of the elderly on learning tasks. These conclusions are based largely on cross-sectional studies of verbal learning comparing older and younger subjects. Longitudinal data are sparse but supportive of the existence of a true learning deficit. It appears that ability in paired-associate learning begins to decline in the 40s and that serial learning declines become significant in the 60s (Arenberg and Robertson-Tchabo 1977). We know little about the reasons for these learning deficits, although it appears that the answers may lie in the areas of memory and information processing (Siegler 1980). Even though the learning literature has not supplied answers regarding the origin of the deficit, it has led to the identification of variables that facilitate learning by the elderly, a contribution of great practical importance.

MEMORY

To review briefly, learning and memory are seen as part of the same process, especially from within the currently dominant information-processing framework. Proponents of this model assume that the learner participates actively, rather than passively, in acquiring and remembering information. Most of the learning literature stems from a stimulus-response viewpoint, but memory researchers in the 1970s used the information-processing approach. Paired-associate and serial-learning tasks are used to study cognitive activities in memory research, just as in the learning studies described above. Use of cross-sectional methods also predominate in both areas of investigation. Memory is currently conceptualized as a system for handling information organized into sequentially related components. The three basic components are known as sensory memory, primary memory, and secondary memory.

Sensory Memory

Information is first registered in sensory memory, a very short-term store (0.25 to 2 seconds) of the most basic environmental information from visual and auditory systems. It is similar to a perceptual process. Unless this information is transferred immediately to the next memory stage, it decays. For example, when we are introduced to someone new, the sensory memory of that person's name is the shortest time required to identify the letters of the new name (Fozard 1980). Attentional processes are particularly important at this stage to get the information coded into the next part of the memory system.

Results of several studies have suggested that older adults need more time than younger adults to identify numerals or digits both individually and in groups (e.g., Walsh and Thompson 1978). Apparently the rate of assimilation of verbal information from sensory memory is not well developed in the elderly. Furthermore, it appears that older subjects are more susceptible than their younger counterparts to disruption of cognitive performance when their attention is divided, perhaps because necessary information was never fully registered in sensory memory (Siegler 1980).

Primary Memory

Assuming proper attention on the part of the subject, some information from sensory memory is transferred into primary memory, where information is coded and organized before being passed on to secondary memory. Primary memory is seen as the control center for memory processing; it reflects the individual's most recent experience. It is very brief, although longer than sensory memory. For example, to continue with Fozard's (1980) illustration involving an introduction, primary memory would be involved in recall of the new name just after hearing it.

To measure primary memory, the subject is usually presented with a string of numbers (digit span), letters, or words and then tested for immediate recall. The capacity of this memory system has been investigated across the life cycle, and few if any changes with age have been noted; at all ages about seven digits can be retained. Based on these findings, it appears that age-related differences in primary memory capacity are minimal. This conclusion has recently been challenged as the result of data that suggest that, when cognitive manipulation is required to reorganize the input, capacity is reduced among older subjects (Hartley, Harker, and Walsh 1980). Nevertheless, primary memory is thought to be the aspect of memory least affected by age-related changes.

Secondary Memory

When material in primary memory is rehearsed, it may be transferred to secondary memory, where material is stored indefinitely. Secondary memory is the highly organized major repository of information no longer in mind. Its capacity, unlike that of primary memory, is unlimited. Secondary memory is characterized by active processing of material in order to fix the information in memory for long periods. To achieve acquisition, new material must be organized and integrated with information already in storage, i.e., it must be made meaningful (Botwinick 1978). To extend the analogy of meeting a new person, secondary memory would come into play when one remembered the original new name after having met ten additional people (Fozard 1980). If the original name could not be remembered the failure would be seen as one of acquisition, storage, or retrieval operations.

Age differences in secondary memory are those best documented in the literature on memory and aging. It has repeatedly been found that younger people perform better once the span of primary memory has been exceeded. Researchers have examined acquisition, storage, and retrieval in secondary memory with young and old adults and have concluded that storage is relatively unaffected by age changes. Therefore, studies have concentrated on acquisition and retrieval. Hartley, Harker, and Walsh (1980) have identified three major areas that have been investigated in the search for factors contributing to the age decrement in secondary memory: (1) acquisition versus retrieval deficiency, (2) organizational processes, and (3) encoding approaches, or levels of processing. We will consider each of these in turn.

Studies examining age differences in acquisition and retrieval have most commonly used measures of recognition and recall. Recognition requires the identification of material to which one has already been exposed; it is thought not to involve retrieval. Recall refers to the extraction of information without the benefit of contextual cues; it is thought to involve retrieval operations. For example, multiple-choice tests require recognition, and essay exams require recall. It was first thought that age differences were present in recall but not in recognition, thus implicating retrieval deficits in old age (e.g., Schonfield 1965). However, when later researchers began to use more difficult tasks, age differences became evident even in recognition memory (e.g., Erber 1974). These data suggest that although retrieval deficits are a major contributor to the age decrement in secondary memory, they are not the only cause. In addition, as Hartley, Harker, and Walsh (1980) pointed out, investigators have realized that it may not be practically possible to differentiate acquisition from retrieval.

We mentioned in the section on learning that the elderly in particular benefit from the provision of mediational techniques in paired-associate learning. This line of evidence, among others, had led to a second area of research concerned with age decrements in secondary memory. It has been hypothesized that organizational processes are deficient in older adults and that this interferes with recall, which requires a higher level of organization than recognition (e.g., Hultsch 1974). Direct measures of the amount of organization carried out by memorizers of different ages have produced inconsistent results. Another approach has examined recall in young and old subjects with tasks of varying intrinsic organizational levels, e.g., lists of related versus unrelated words (Laurence 1967). As predicted, age differences were reduced in recall of lists of related words, indicating that the elderly benefited more from the built-in organization. The final approach involved instructing younger and older adults to use organizational strategies (Hultsch 1974). Results of these studies were mixed. Thus, the notion that elderly people suffer from an organizational deficit that leads to age decrements in secondary memory has received only partial support (Hartley, Harker, and Walsh 1980).

The third major focus of research on aging and memory is based on the concept of memory as a continuum within which different levels of processing occur (Craik and Lockhart 1972). This approach emphasizes a close examination of encoding operations. In the level-of-processing model, memory is thought to be directly related to the depth at which material is processed and the amount of processing performed at that level. Depth refers to degree of encoding or organization of material. The elderly are thought to exhibit less depth of processing than young adults. Studies of this hypothesis have revealed that although deeper encoding does result in more effective acquisition, it does not necessarily lead to retrieval of the material. Young subjects seem to benefit more from deeper processing than elderly subjects do (Eysenck 1974). It is not yet clear whether older adults are in fact less able than younger adults to process at deep levels, or whether older people can be taught to use strategies that enhance deeper processing.

Current Developments and Summary

The field of aging and memory is currently in a state of rapid development and is moving in several promising new directions. One of these is age differences in prose recall, involving tasks closer to those required in daily living than paired-associate and serial learning. Other research focuses on the amelioration of the memory deficits that many older people experience. Some investigators are evaluating the effects of various drugs on memory; others are developing and examining the results of memory-training programs with elderly trainees. Unfortunately, these and other attempts to overcome processing deficits have usually not completely closed the memory gap between older and younger adults. Several researchers are now asserting that processing strategies among elderly people are not the major cause of age decrements. They suggest that a slowed speed of processing, based on physiological changes, can account for age changes. These are just a few of the lines of investigation currently being pursued.

In summary, there is some experimental evidence for an age decrement in sensory memory, and virtually all types of evidence indicate an age decrement in secondary memory. On the other hand, primary memory is thought to continue relatively unchanged through later adulthood. Deficient processing strategies do not appear to fully explain memory deficits in the elderly, and a number of promising leads are being vigorously pursued by current researchers.

SPEED OF BEHAVIOR

One reviewer of the literature on aging concluded that "in studies of age-related behavioral change, the observed slowing of behavior is the most consistent finding: across wide ranges of behavior, from simple motor movements to complex cognitive process, and from the earliest studies starting with Galton in the 1880s up to the current research findings" (Siegler 1980, p. 176). When measured in the laboratory, speed of response for elderly subjects is quantitatively, but not qualitatively, different from that for young adults. This slowing of behavior in older age is thought important because it reflects age-related changes in the central nervous system. Also, it has consequences for a number of other behaviors, including learning and memory, intelligence, and even physiological and cellular system processes. Given the broad general importance of speed of behavior, a variety of methods have been used to study it, including measures from psychophysiology, decision making, and motor performance.

Peripheral Versus Central Nervous System Changes

A major question has been whether loss of speed with age is due to changes in peripheral or in central processing systems. Location of the cause in peripheral systems such as the sense organs or neuromuscular pathways would be of less importance because these do not have much effect on cognition and perception (Botwinick 1978). However, if changes in the central nervous system were found to be the cause, this would have major effects, as mentioned above, on other behaviors.

A number of investigators have studied the contribution of peripheral factors to loss of speed with age. In an early study, Birren and Botwinick (1955) presented younger and older adults with a task that involved judging which of two bars was longer. Subjects were to respond as quickly as possible by saying "right" or "left." Results indicated that the older were slower than the younger subjects at every level of response difficulty. The age difference was especially pronounced when the discrimination between the two bars was most difficult. The finding that the older group was slower even when the task was easy supported the notion of some causative factor other than perceptual variables. These results and those of other studies on sensory-perceptual factors have led to the conclusion that such factors alone are unable to account for most of the slowing seen with age.

In studies with human subjects that have sought to identify central nervous system changes that contribute to slowing, many investigators have used reaction time as a measure. In reaction-time experiments, a warning signal is given to inform the subject that the stimulus will appear shortly. By manipulating this "preparatory interval" between the warning and the stimulus, researchers have been able to examine the effect on reaction time of variations in states of readiness and of time available to prepare the response. Results of reaction-time studies have suggested that with increasing age, subjects experience more difficulty maintaining an optimal state of readiness to respond. Also, organization of the response is less efficient in the elderly when only a brief period is provided for this.

In order to investigate more specifically possible central nervous system effects of slowing on cognition and perception, more complex reaction-time tasks have been devised in which choices are involved in the required response. Generally, choice reaction-time studies demonstrate among the elderly an increasing and disproportionate slowness in response time as the number of choices increases (Botwinick 1978). However, this pattern is seen only when the duration of the exposure of the stimulus is long; when it is brief, elderly people react as young adults do. This differential responding suggests that older adults may be more cautious than the younger and for this reason take more time than necessary. Motivation, another noncognitive variable, has also been suggested as an influence on choice reaction time that is more important for older than for younger subjects. Evidence for this hypothesis lies in data that indicate that on some reaction-time trials, elderly subjects respond as fast as or faster than their younger counterparts. Siegler (1980) pointed out that older people who are performing near the limit of their ability may not be motivated to keep up such a high level of effort.

A General Mediating Process

Birren, Woods, and Williams (1980) reviewed the literature regarding the effects of a number of health-related variables on the age decrement in response speed. They concluded that the biological fitness of the individual is directly related to speed of behavior and suggested that measures of speed may provide a useful indication of a person's biological functioning. Birren, Woods, and Williams envisioned a general mediating process in the central nervous system that leads to a slowing of behavior with age and that in turn may be seen across many specific behaviors.

A similar view was expressed by Cerella, Poon, & Williams (1980). They put forward the idea of a "complexity hypothesis" and defined it as follows: "The magnitude of the age difference in reaction times is proportional to the difficulty of the task" (p. 333). Some of the evidence for this hypothesis was presented above, indicating that the elderly exhibit a greater deficit when the task is more complex. Cerella, Poon, and Williams used data from eighteen previous studies to test their hypothesis and found that it was supported. They also found that a "uniform slowing of mental functions" (p. 339) occurred and that there appeared to be two levels of deficit. On the sensorimotor level, there was a small deficit; on the cognitive level, a more marked slowing was seen. Therefore, the difficulty of the task was not the important factor, as there was a uniform deficit across the range of tasks on each level. They concluded that the important factor is the major involvement of the central nervous system rather than peripheral processes. This is interpreted as support for the complexity hypothesis, with two levels only: central and peripheral. In other words, whereas some theories explain complexity effects in terms of factors that are present in difficult tasks only, this theory indicates that there is a single mechanism affecting equally performance on difficult and easy tasks, a slowing in the performance of information processing.

Influence of Noncognitive Variables

Another area of research in aging and speed of behavior has concerned interventions designed to overcome the deficits shown by the elderly. First, it should be noted that there is a great deal of variability and overlap between people of different ages in speed of behavior. Many elderly people are quicker in their responses than many younger adults (Botwinick 1980). Some evidence suggests that slowing with age may be reduced through physical exercise. Practice also appears to decrease the degree of slowing seen in later life. Motivational factors, cautiousness, and biological fitness have already been mentioned as factors that may influence speed of behavior, especially among the elderly. As yet none of these interventions has reliably brought older adults up to the quick performance times shown by younger subjects, but the magnitude of the age differences has been significantly decreased.

Summary

In summary, speed of behavior slows with age, and this seems to reflect a process occurring in the central nervous system. On sensorimotor tasks, only a small difference is seen in speed between young and old adults. On more complex, cognitive tasks, a significant decline in speed is found for elderly as compared to younger subjects. A number of factors, such as health, motivation, exercise, and practice, have been found to influence the age decrement in speed of behavior.

INTELLIGENCE

The cognitive processes we have discussed thus far are all involved in what is known as intelligence. It is not possible to directly observe and measure intelligence; rather, estimates of intellectual ability must be made from observed behaviors that are thought to reflect intelligence, an abstract construct. As a result, there has been a great deal of controversy over the years concerning the nature of intelligence and the best ways to observe and measure it. It is not surprising that the existence and/or extent of intellectual decline with age is also controversial. Although different types of measurement and varying types of research methods have led to contradictory findings on the relationships between intelligence and age, several trends have emerged. In a comprehensive review of the literature, Botwinick (1977) concluded that intellectual ability is maintained up through the 50s and 60s, with decrements becoming more common in old age. He also found that verbal abilities hold up significantly longer than nonverbal abilities and that the age decrement is first noted on those tasks that require quick performance. In addition, people who perform well when young will also perform well when old.

Currently intelligence is viewed as a composite of a number of different abilities that have developed within the individual as a result of genetic and environmental factors. Wechsler's definition (in Matarazzo 1972, p. 79) shows that intelligence is thought of as a combination of general and specific abilities:

> Intelligence, as a hypothetical construct, is the aggregate or global capacity of the individual to act purposefully, to think rationally, and to deal effectively with his environment. It is aggregate or global because it is composed of elements or abilities (features) which, although not entirely independent, are qualitatively differentiable. By measurement of these abilities through scores from a test (such as the WAIS [Wechsler Adult Intelligence Scale]), we have available to us objective data which are invaluable in the evaluation of intelligence. But functional intelligence is not identical with the mere sum of these abilities, however inclusive. There are three important reasons for this: (1) The ultimate products of intelligent behavior are a function not only of the number of abilities or their quality but also of the way in which they are combined, that is, their configuration. (2) Factors other than intellectual ability, for example, those of drive and incentive, are involved in intelligent behavior. (3) Finally, whereas different orders of intelligent behavior may require varying degrees of intellectual ability, an excess of any given ability may add relatively little to the effectiveness of the behavior as a whole.

There have been two major approaches to the study of intelligence. The psychometric approach has to do with testing and measurement, whereas proponents of the cognitive approach study intelligence as it is reflected in processes such as memory and problem-solving. This section will be more concerned with psychometric issues, as specific processes are covered in other sections.

Assessment

Several tests have been used to gather most of the data on adult intelligence. The best known of these is the WAIS (Matarazzo 1972), which comprises eleven subtests measuring different abilities. The subtests can be divided into those that measure verbal and those that measure performance aspects of intelligence. Verbal intelligence appears to increase until the 60s and then gradually decline, while performance skills increase until the 40s, gradually fall off until the 60s, and then decline more sharply (Siegler 1980). The verbally oriented subtests have been termed "age-insensitive" by Botwinick (1978); they measure stored information and general verbal ability. The "age-sensitive" performance subtests assess psychomotor skills, and most are timed, requiring a speedy performance for a higher score.

Another distinction is that between "fluid" and "crystallized" intelligence (e.g., Horn and Cattell 1966). In this model it is proposed that fluid intelligence consists of such abilities as reasoning, figural relations, and memory tasks that are seen as tied to biological aging because of their neurological basis. Crystallized intelligence, however, is the product of the action of fluid intelligence on the environment and can be defined generally as knowledge. Fluid intelligence is roughly analogous to the performance skills assessed by such tests as the WAIS, and crystallized intelligence seems related to the verbal subtests. Not surprisingly, fluid intelligence has been found to decrease with age, while crystallized intelligence appears to remain constant or increase (Horn 1975).

Much of the controversy previously alluded to concerning the extent of the age decrement in intellectual abilities can be traced to problems associated with commonly used research methods. For a discussion of these problems, see the section "Methodology" in Chapter 1. Unfortunately, although progress is being made using these designs, Botwinick (1978) noted that they are often used incorrectly at present.

Noncognitive Variables and Plasticity

A number of noncognitive factors affect performance of elderly people on intelligence tests. Again, health status is an important moderator, especially if a health problem is brain-related, such as hypertension or arteriosclerosis. Sensory losses such as hearing loss also affect test performance, as do environmental losses that lead to increased isolation and to decreased intellectual stimulation. Level of formal education is closely tied to level of test performance, probably because intelligence tests were devised to predict school achievement.

Recently there has been an increased emphasis on the "plasticity" of intelligence in old age, i.e., intraindividual variability. Willis and Baltes (1980) noted that the traditional psychometric approach has focused on intellectual abilities as largely invariant and fixed, which has led to the assumption that an individual's test score reflects his or her potential. In their criticism of this model they asserted that "this is a highly questionable inference . . . , because it involves generalization from performance in test situations to unobserved settings and to possible treatment benefits and thereby neglects intraindividual variability" (p. 265). Using this alternative viewpoint, several researchers are currently conducting studies that explore the plasticity of older adult intellectual performance in response to performance-enhancing treatments. It is too early to reach firm conclusions, but under conditions in which supportive conditions are provided or in which the elderly attend to the tasks involved, they do appear to benefit (Willis and Baltes 1980).

Another current area of interest concerns a phenomenon known as "terminal drop." It appears that people who exhibit a rapid "drop" in cognitive test scores are at higher risk of death than those who score about as they had before. Siegler (1980) reviewed the literature, which is mixed, and concluded that "while intelligence is not the only correlate of survival, it appears to be a significant one" (p. 185). The terminal-drop hypothesis highlights the importance of the relationship between cognitive functioning and health in later adulthood. The specific nature of this relationship remains to be explored.

Summary

In summary, intellectual abilities are thought to be stable until the 50s and 60s, at which time certain abilities decline. Individuals who perform well when young tend to perform well when old. Noncognitive variables such as health affect the intellectual test performance of the elderly, and a new view of this performance as plastic or modifiable is becoming more commonly accepted.

PROBLEM-SOLVING

The study of problem-solving in late adulthood is closely related to the study of intelligence. Problem-solving requires reasoning, concept learning, memory, and so on, all of which are abilities involved in intelligence-test performance. Studies of problem-solving use various types of difficult, usually abstract, problems. Surprisingly, in his review of this literature, Botwinick (1978) concluded that "some types of intelligence are related to some types of problem-solving ability, but not all" (p. 237). Nevertheless, it is always important to match young and old subjects on intelligence in studies of problem-solving.

Older adults perform better on concrete problem-solving tasks than on abstract, although this distinction lessens when the older individual is more highly educated (e.g., Arenberg 1968; Botwinick 1978). It also appears that the developmental pattern of ability to solve problems may be different for meaningful, concrete problems and for traditional abstract problems. In a recent study, Denney and Palmer (1981) found that, on abstract problems, task performance decreased gradually across the adult years. However, on meaningful practical problems, performance peaked in middle age and declined thereafter.

A cognitive variable that has been found to affect problem-solving in later adulthood is that of inflexibility of thought, or rigidity. Elderly people experience more difficulty than younger adults when the task requires shifting from one kind of problem to another. Older subjects also have more trouble when redundant information is presented along with that necessary to solve the problem. For example, Hoyer, Rebok, and Sved (1979) reported that, as the number of irrelevant dimensions presented on a unidimensional problem-solving task increased, older adults made more errors than young and middle-aged adults. Apparently the organizational strategies of elderly problem-solvers are not as effective as those of young adults. In addition to the evidence just mentioned, a group of studies indicates that the inquiries older subjects make for information during problem-solving tend to be repetitive and disorganized compared to those of younger subjects (Botwinick 1978). Research has not yet determined what specific processes elderly people engage in during problem-solving, and, although some conclusions can be drawn, there are numerous equivocal and conflicting outcomes (Giambra and Arenberg 1980).

Compared to research with other cognitive variables, studies on problem-solving and aging are sparse. In a recent review of studies since 1974, Giambra and Arenberg (1980) concluded that minimal advances had been made in the 1970s and suggested several modifications they believed would enhance the usefulness of research in this area. Their suggestions included using paradigms with elderly people that have proved fruitful with younger adults; having subjects "think aloud" in order to make accessible their thought processes; and studying fewer subjects over a wider range of problems.

Results of cross-sectional and longitudinal studies indicate that general problem-solving ability, like intelligence, is stable until the 50s or 60s, with no real decrement until the 70s. Again, there is a great deal of inter-individual variability, and some subjects show no decrement in late adulthood. Plasticity, or intraindividual variation, is an issue in problem-solving research as it is with intellectual abilities in old age. Early cognitive-training programs designed to teach various problem-solving skills found short-term improvement on experimental tasks. Later training programs have also garnered evidence for long-term improvement (e.g., Labouvie-Vief and Gonda 1976). Problem-solving is yet another area in which cognitive-skill training holds promise for the future.

In summary, problem-solving ability decreases in later adulthood, but an individual's performance may vary from this norm. Areas in which particular problems for elderly people have been found include abstract problems, shifting from one kind of problem to another, problems in which redundant information is presented, and problems that demand requesting and organizing necessary information. Cognitive-skill training programs have been developed to improve older adults' performance; they have found plasticity of performance on problem-solving tasks.

SUMMARY AND CONCLUSIONS

In this chapter we examined the relationship between cognitive processes and age. Cognitive abilities usually decline in varying degrees in later adulthood, especially in advanced old age. It must be emphasized that an individual's performance may fluctuate from these norms, and some elderly people do not experience noticeable decrements in cognitive performance.

Central nervous system changes have been implicated as underlying causes of cognitive losses, although other factors contribute. For example, health is an important determinant of cognitive functioning in old age, with poor health closely related to lower functioning. Recently, the plasticity of cognitive abilities has been investigated, and programs designed to improve cognitive performance have benefited elderly participants.

6

PSYCHOSOCIAL ASPECTS
OF LATER ADULTHOOD

We have stressed that aging is a multidimensional process in which biological, psychological, and social factors interact to determine each individual's unique course through the life cycle. In this chapter we use the term "psychosocial" to refer to aspects of later adulthood that involve an especially close relationship between psychological and social variables. Given the constant change implicit in the developmental approach to adulthood, it is to be expected that the psychosocial processes in old age are usually concerned with adaptation to some form of change. Issues considered here include effects of age on personality; adaptation to later adulthood, including relocation and retirement; characteristics of families in old age; and coping with dying and with bereavement. These topics provide a very modest introduction to psychosocial gerontology, a major focus of aging research.

PERSONALITY IN LATER ADULTHOOD

In earlier chapters we presented theories of adult development, several of which extend into old age. These theories provide an introduction to the general developmental tasks many people face during various stages of life and as such are useful when considering personality in later adulthood, as personality may be thought of as an interaction between the individual and the environment (Mischel 1968). Although the environment does affect some aspects of personality, research has generally found personality to be stable across the life span. One exception is interiority. As people age, they gradually become more inner-oriented, turning inward and away from active life involvements (Neugarten 1977). This finding has led to the development of the disengagement theory of adaptation to aging (Cumming and Henry 1961), which will be discussed shortly. First, in order to illustrate several areas in which research is being conducted on personality variables and aging, we will summarize the literature on locus of control, self-concept, and sex-role behaviors.

Locus of control (Rotter 1966) refers to a belief system regarding the effects of one's actions on the outcome of events, with internal locus of control referring to a belief in personal ability to affect outcomes and external locus of control referring to a belief that fate or others are responsible for what happens. With younger adults, locus of control has been linked to numerous variables, among them achievement, reactions to hospitalization and to types of psychological treatments, adaptation to other transitions, and self-concept. In a review of the literature, Siegler (1980) concluded that locus of control is stable across the life span until age 60, at which time subjects either shift toward externality or remain unchanged. Until age 60 older adults are as internal as college students. A major area of interest has been the relationship between internal or external locus of control and adaptation in old age. For example, Kuypers (1972) reported that internal older subjects adapted better than externals to the environment. However, as Zarit (1980) pointed out, internality was associated with intelligence, and therefore it could not be ascertained whether higher internality or higher intelligence enhanced adaptation. Other studies have found that the environment of the individual is important in determining the adaptive efficacy of internality versus externality. For institutionalized persons it seems that externality is more adaptive (Felton and Kahana 1974). Reporting on her own work, Siegler (1980) suggested that some components of locus of control remain stable across different environments and experiences while others change. She is currently investigating the nature of these relationships.

Studies of self-concept examine the ways in which people see themselves. This variable appears to be stable through the adult years. Monge (1975) assessed the self-concepts of people aged 9 to 98 and reported that the same basic factors in self-concept applied across all ages. Based on the findings of Schwartz and Kleemeier (1965), however, it appears that variables such as health status can have a major effect on self-concept. They measured self-concept in young and old subjects. Each age group was divided so that half were healthy and half were suffering from significant health problems. Differences in responses were found on the healthy versus ill dimension, but not on the age dimension. These results underscore the need for further research on the relationship between health, age, and personality.

The study of changes in sex-role behaviors with age is complicated by the changing nature of sex roles in today's society (Troll and Parron 1981). Despite this confounding factor, it does appear that, at least for some people, sex-role changes occur in the adult years. The general pattern of these changes is toward increased "androgyny," a balanced combination of masculine and feminine behaviors, with women becoming more autonomous and men more expressive. This shift toward androgyny seems to be more difficult for women, largely because of cultural values. As Huyck (1976) noted, dominant older women are often feared, disliked, and labeled negatively, e.g., "old witch" or "old battle-ax," whereas the kindly old man is a more acceptable figure.

Increased androgyny has been linked to better mental health in young and middle-aged adults. For example, Livson (1976) found in a sample of 50-year-old men and women that most were reviving characteristics of opposite-sex behavior that had not been used since childhood. Independent ratings indicated that those people who shifted their sex-role behaviors were better at coping in general than those who remained inflexible. These changes, as assessed in longitudinal studies such as Livson's (1976), do not result in crisis or upheaval; rather, it is the lack of such changes that is associated with problems. The flexibility of increased androgyny appears to contribute to better adjustment to stresses in general and aging in particular (Sinnott 1977).

COPING WITH AND ADAPTATION TO AGING

Personality and Adaptation

Adaptation to later adulthood has been studied from a number of different perspectives, including the theories of adult development and specific personality variables already mentioned. Another approach involves the examination of various personality types and their relationship to successful adaptation. Two studies in this area stand out in particular. Reichard, Livson, and Peterson (1962) studied eighty-seven men over age 55. They obtained evidence for five basic personality types. The best-adjusted men were termed *mature* and could accept themselves and grow old with few regrets. The *rocking-chair* men were also relatively well-adjusted and viewed old age as a time of freedom from responsibility and a time for leisure activities. Moderately well adjusted were the *armored* men, who protected themselves against anxiety by keeping busy. The *angry* men had adjusted poorly, were bitter, and blamed others for their problems. The other group of poorly adjusted men was the *self-haters*, who were depressed rather than angry and blamed themselves for their failures. Reichard, Livson, and Peterson concluded that adaptation in old age was related to personality type in younger adulthood, not to age, and that this personality style was relatively stable into later adulthood.

The second study of interest was conducted by Neugarten, Havighurst, and Tobin (1968) with a sample of men and women aged 70 to 79. The investigators explored the relationships between personality characteristics, social activities, and happiness and came up with four major personality types: integrated, armored-defended, passive-dependent, and unintegrated. Their results were generally consistent with those of Reichard (1962), both in the broad types identified and in the finding that adjustment was related to personality type rather than to age. People who were happier with themselves and who had positive evaluations of their lives adapted better.

Successful Adaptation to Aging

The question whether an active or a disengaged life-style is more predictive of good adjustment represents a major area of research and controversy in the literature on adaptation to aging. In an early cross-sectional study, Cumming and Henry (1961) examined the activity levels of healthy persons living in the community and concluded that, starting in late middle age, people decreased their social involvement and activities and gradually "disengaged" from society. Their disengagement theory views this process as an adaptive one that facilitates the individual's ability to cope with losses and declines in old age. Other theorists disagreed with this interpretation based on research results that indicated that more socially active elderly people were better adjusted (e.g., Neugarten, Havighurst, and Tobin 1968). This viewpoint has been termed activity theory.

Taken as a whole, the experimental literature on the activity-disengagement debate indicates that neither high nor low activity level alone is associated with better adaptation, although most studies find a decline in activity level with age. Zarit (1980) suggested that a more useful way to assess successful coping would be to look at the difference between the activities an individual currently engages in and those she or he would like to engage in. This approach takes into account individual differences and allows for the impact of such variables as health. The definition of successful adaptation as a balance between what one can do and what one would like to do then eliminates the need to argue activity versus disengagement. Either extreme is likely to lead to maladaptive coping, and most gerontologists now agree that the debate is an overly simplistic one.

Health is an important variable that is often overlooked in studies of adaptation. Its relevance was highlighted in a review of 30 years of research on the variable "subjective well-being" (Larson 1978), a variable often thought to reflect adaptation to old age. Health was the variable most closely related to subjective well-being among the elderly, followed by socioeconomic status and then by social interaction. Care must be taken in equating subjective well-being, or morale, with adaptation, however; Zarit (1980) reviewed several problems with this assumption.

Another way in which adaptation in later adulthood has been studied involves looking at older people as they face specific transitions, such as relocation. The work on relocation has usually been concerned with a move to an institutional setting from the community or from another institutional facility. Results of these studies suggest that even the very old have a remarkable capacity for adaptation. Also, researchers have identified variables that are associated with successful and unsuccessful adaptation after the move. For example, Lieberman (1975) examined people undergoing both types of relocation just mentioned and assessed coping ability, cognitive variables, personality variables, and physical functioning. He found that the most important factor in determining difficulty in coping was the amount of change required by the individual. In addition, those people who were functioning at low cognitive and physical levels were unable to adapt. However, high levels of functioning did not necessarily lead to successful coping. Several personality traits were closely related to positive adaptation, including being aggressive, irritating, narcissistic, and demanding. Apparently, it is not so much that people develop these traits with age, but rather that people who already possess them tend to survive more successfully.

In a related study, Tobin and Lieberman (1976) interviewed and administered tests to a group of people on waiting lists to enter nursing homes and again two months and one year after institutionalization. Their results indicated that many psychological changes thought to take place as a result of institutionalization, such as feeling abandoned, actually had occurred before the elderly entered the nursing home. They also found that functioning during the first two months in the nursing home remained stable. Passivity was the psychological variable most closely related to serious loss of functioning and death.

Although the adaptive abilities of the elderly appear to be more effective than previously thought, researchers have found that relocation, especially from community to institution, is associated with an increase in health problems and in deaths (Bourestom and Pastalan 1981). Recently researchers have attempted to mitigate these effects by preparing people for the move and by helping them feel more control over the transition (Schulz and Brenner 1977). Although these interventions are laudable and may eventually enhance the lives of many institutionalized elderly people, Zarit (1980) suggested that preference be given to determining alternatives to institutional care.

RETIREMENT

Research on the various aspects of retirement constitutes a major area of gerontology. Here only those studies that are most relevant to adaptation will be covered. Attitudes toward retirement are generally positive, although cross-sectional studies indicate that as people approach retirement age, attitudes become less favorable and the preferred age for retirement rises (Goudy, Powers, Keith, and Reger 1980). Attitudes are also related to income level, with those making more money expressing more favorable attitudes. Contrary to expectation, these people are actually less likely than others to retire early, probably because of their greater commitment to their jobs (Atchley 1980). People at lower income levels are worried about finances and tend to continue to work for this reason. Generally, the higher the expected retirement income, the more positive the attitude toward retirement.

Factors That Influence Timing of Retirement

Most workers retire as soon as it is financially possible to do so. Therefore, the decision is when to retire, not whether to retire. This is illustrated by the finding that the typical retirement age dropped from 65 to 63 when Social Security benefits became available at age 62 instead of 65. A number of factors that influence the decision of when to retire have been reviewed by Atchley (1980). Many older adults who lose their jobs are unable to find new employment. Hiring policies tend to discriminate against older workers, with employers claiming that older people do not meet the physical or skill requirements of the jobs, an allegation that Atchley concluded is unsubstantiated. Another factor is the incentive that some companies provide to workers to retire after a certain number of years of employment. Mandatory retirement is a third factor that affects varying percentages of the labor force, depending on the type of job. Reno (1972) found that 56% of professional and technical workers were subject to mandatory retirement, compared to 23% of service workers. However, the percentages of workers who were actually forced to retire because of these regulations were much smaller, as most people retire voluntarily prior to age 65 or 70.

Health is a factor often cited by workers as the major reason for retirement, and it is undoubtedly important. It is not known, though, how many people cite health reasons in order to make retirement more socially acceptable. Retirement is viewed positively and acceptingly by assembly-line workers, for example, but professionals tend to have a negative bias toward it. Other factors are attitudes of friends and family, and pressure put on the worker by the employer.

Adaptation to Retirement

The ability of people to cope with retirement is related to their preretirement attitudes and expectations. Those who have more positive attitudes and expectations are more likely to adapt successfully. In a longitudinal study, Streib and Schneider (1971) found that, 4 to 6 years after retirement, 30% of their respondents reported that retirement was a more positive experience than they had expected and only 4 to 5% reported a more negative experience. Contrary to popular belief, retirement does not lead to increased mortality. Declines in health are related to age, not retirement, and it has even been found that unskilled workers experience a slight improvement in health after retirement (Streib and Schneider 1971). In the same study it was also found that life satisfaction was not affected by retirement. Generally, the subjective evaluation of the effects of retirement is affected more by variables such as family situation, health, and income than by the fact of retirement itself.

Adaptation to retirement is also related to occupation. Simpson and McKinney (1972) found that white-collar and skilled blue-collar workers adjusted better to retirement than unskilled blue-collar workers. Professional workers especially may opt to participate in activities related to their work after retirement and may thus continue to enjoy much of the status they had and to work in an unrestricted manner (McKenzie 1980). Some of these differences between occupations may be due to income, as people in higher-level occupations are more financially secure, and this security is linked to successful retirement.

Regarding the effects of personality on adaptation to retirement, the findings are essentially the same as those discussed previously for personality and adaptation to old age. If a person has coped successfully with earlier life transitions, it is likely that he or she will adjust successfully to retirement. For some people, successful retirement may mean sitting quietly at home, while for others it may involve a whirl of social activities. Once again, the importance of viewing each older person as a unique individual becomes evident.

THE FAMILY IN LATER ADULTHOOD

Marriage

Among people aged 65 and over, about 80% of the men and 40% of the women were married in 1975 (Atchley and Miller 1980), which means that about 50% of the population consisted of married couples. However, by age 80 to 84, only 29% were married, and this proportion continued to decrease steadily with age. The declining rate is due mainly to higher mortality rates and to the shorter life expectancy of men. Most people who are widowed in later adulthood do not remarry.

Although there is little longitudinal evidence, cross-sectional studies indicate that marital satisfaction is higher in later adulthood than in some periods of earlier adulthood, particularly middle age. Lee (1978) reported that only health was more important than marital satisfaction for older married men when predicting overall life satisfaction. For women, marital satisfaction ranked first. The importance of these findings is highlighted when one considers that for both men and women marital satisfaction was a better predictor of life satisfaction than age, standard of living, or whether or not the person was retired.

Married couples seem to shift in their relationships with each other in old age toward more emotionally expressive styles and toward more interest in each other's personalities (Thurnher 1975). They spend less time with family and friends compared to widowed or never-married elderly people, and marriage tends to be the focal point of their lives (Atchley 1980). Sharing of activities increases once all children have left the home, and the relationship can often be described as one of equality, relative to the sex-role behaviors and divisions of labor seen among younger couples. This is especially true of happily married older adults.

A great deal of evidence suggests that marriage can mitigate many of the negative experiences associated with later adulthood. Unfortunately, although many widowed people would like to remarry, it is much more difficult for women than men to do so. By age 70 a majority of older women are widows, but this is not true for men until age 85 (Atchley 1980), due to the tendency of women to marry men older than they are and the longer life expectancy of women. Men are therefore much more likely to remarry than women are, with the desire for companionship being the reason most frequently given by members of both sexes (McKain 1969).

Relationships with Children

In their review of older people and their adult children, Atchley and Miller (1980) summarized the results of areas of research known as residential proximity, interaction frequency, mutual aid, and qualitative aspects of the relationships. With regard to residential proximity, they found evidence that as children reach middle age and settle down, and as some older parents move after retirement, there seems to be a convergence of residences so that parents and children end up living closer together than they did when children were young adults. Interaction frequency is high between parents and adult children. For example, Harris and Associates (1975) in their survey of older adults found that 55% had seen one of their children within the last 24 hours and 81% within the last 2 weeks. Mutual aid refers to help provided by either parents or children, such as child care, financial support, or moral support. In a majority of studies it has been found that aid did flow in both directions and that parents with adequate physical and financial resources gave more help to their children than they received. Parents who were poor, in poor health, widowed, or divorced received more help from children in samples of both black and white respondents. Overall, parents continue to provide help to their children as long as they can.

Research on the qualitative aspects of relationships has focused on the feelings involved. Atchley and Miller (1980) concluded that feelings are usually positive between parents and children and that relationships are best when parents are able to be independent. Despite the stresses that may occur when parents become dependent, most children carry out their responsibilities and care for their parents. Interestingly, although studies of disengagement have found that some people gradually detach themselves from many aspects of life, older people rarely disengage from their children. Children remain important to parents, and parents to children, throughout the life span.

Other Relatives and Friends

Next to spouses and children, siblings are the most important relations for the elderly, and many siblings grow closer in later adulthood. Very little research has been conducted on sibling relationships in old age. What little there is suggests, as would be expected, that relationships in early life affect the likelihood that siblings will become close later on. Nieces, nephews, and cousins may provide additional important relationships for an elderly individual.

Friends, although not as important as spouses and children, may also serve as important sources of contact with the outside world and of support. Most people report a decrease in number of friends with age (Atchley 1980), partly because of the difficulty of replacing lost friendships. Friends tend to be of the same age, sex, marital status, and socioeconomic class. How many there are depends on a number of factors, such as how long the older individual has lived in the neighborhood and how many elderly people there are in the immediate vicinity. Many studies have documented the importance of friends in the daily lives of the elderly. One illustration is the finding of Lowenthal and Havens (1968) that the presence of even one confidant, or person with whom one has a close relationship, serves as an effective buffer against the stresses of retirement and widowhood.

DEATH: THE PATIENT AND THE FAMILY

Death

Until very recently, death was an occurrence most people were familiar with. Deaths were more evenly distributed across the life cycle, and most people died at home. Nowadays, 80% of those who die are over age 65, and a majority die in hospitals and nursing homes. As a result, most of the population in Western society is insulated from the reality of death, and attitudes toward death have become characterized by fear and denial. Evidence for this is all around: Euphemisms are used to refer to death ("passed on"), anxiety is associated with attending funerals, many people refuse to make wills or arrange for their own funerals, cemeteries are shunned, external signs of mourning are minimized, and so on.

Elderly people seem to think about death more often but to experience less fear of death than younger adults (Kalish 1976). Fear of death can be broken down into several components, with the relative importance of each varying from person to person. Included are fears of physical suffering, humiliation, impact on survivors, punishment after death, no longer existing, and death of others (Schulz 1978).

The denial of death can refer both to the belief that people continue to "experience" after death, such as belief in an afterlife, and to the belief that personal death is distant even after the person is told that it may be imminent (Atchley 1980). For example, many physicians have had the experience of telling an individual he or she has a terminal illness only to return soon thereafter and find the patient acting as though nothing had happened, even denying having been told about the illness.

Health professionals are not immune to fear and denial of death. It is a well-established finding that both physicians and nurses avoid patients once they begin to die (e.g., Kastenbaum and Aisenberg 1972). The training of health professionals contributes to this avoidance by emphasizing an attitude of "detached concern" toward the patient (Lief and Fox 1963) and by focusing on saving lives to the exclusion of dealing with those patients defined as terminal. A patient's death is often equated with failure and disappointment. Furthermore, death sensitizes professionals to the eventuality of their own death and the death of loved ones.

Given this avoidance of dying patients, it is not surprising that physicians also avoid telling patients that they have a terminal illness. The evidence clearly indicates that a majority of physicians do not tell patients that they are dying (Schulz 1978). Reasons given for not informing patients usually have to do with fostering hope and sparing the patient emotional pain, but there is some evidence that an additional reason may be the physician's discomfort. Caldwell and Mishara (1972) interviewed a group of medical doctors concerning their attitudes toward dying patients. All agreed the patient has the right to know that her or his diagnosis is terminal, but only a small minority said they actually tell patients. Nurses apparently also learn to cope with death by avoiding or denying it. Kastenbaum and Aisenberg (1972) reported that nurses were most likely to respond to patients' statements about death with some form of avoidance, such as false reassurance or changing the subject.

The behavior of nurses and physicians is at variance with advice provided by a number of medical experts concerning the advisability of telling a patient his or her diagnosis. Most agree that patients benefit from being told the truth and that the physician owes this to the patient. Hinton (1967) pointed out that a person who suspects the true diagnosis but who is denied the opportunity to discuss it is in fact cruelly isolated, both from staff and from family. He went on to note that "while doctors are trying to judge their patients' capacity to stand unpleasant news, many patients are equally making their intuitive judgments of whether their doctor can bear sincere but difficult questions" (p. 63). In addition, surveys reveal that a large majority of both healthy and terminally ill people want to be told the true diagnosis. Investigations of terminally ill patients who have been told their diagnosis have found no long-term negative effects (Schulz 1978).

In an excellent essay, Brody (1981) effectively demolished the claim that the practice of "benign deception" is worthwhile because it allows the patient to maintain hope. He asserted that hope is more resilient than medical staff realize and that it is possible to tell the patient the truth and at the same time instill a sense of hope. He conculed that "there is no fundamental conflict between our moral duty to preserve hope—to heal our patients with our words and not just with our medicines—and our moral duty to respect our patients as adult human beings who should be given the information they need to make their own free choices about their lives" (p. 1412).

The reluctance of health professionals, dying patients, and their families to discuss death and dying leads to an odd type of interaction that appears slightly unreal to those not involved. This interaction has to do with pretending that the patient is not dying, a "mutual pretense" in which topics pertaining to death are avoided and everyone tries hard to act as though nothing unusual were happening (Glaser and Strauss 1965). When one of the parties involved tried to break through the pretense, others will hasten to prolong it with statements such as, "Don't be silly! You're going to get well." Such efforts to avoid the obvious preclude any real communication among all involved and interfere with the working through of feelings that facilitate successful coping with death and dying. Much has been written about the negative effects of mutual pretense on dying individuals and their families.

Dying

Several theorists have proposed that dying people pass through stages in their adaptation to imminent death. By far the best known of these theorists is Elisabeth Kubler-Ross (1969), who outlined five stages: denial, anger, bargaining, depression, and acceptance. She does not claim that every patient will pass through each stage in order, but rather that the course followed and the number of stages experienced are unique to each person. Unfortunately, the usefulness of this theory is limited by the subjective and ambiguous manner in which data were collected. Nevertheless, Kubler-Ross did alert many people to the fact that there are ways to adapt to dying and that health professionals can assist in this process. Researchers using more objective methods have found that dying patients characteristically become depressed and perhaps anxious about dying, but results are mixed concerning other emotional factors.

Houpt (1979) emphasized the importance of the grief process in the dying patient, a notion that gains support from the findings just mentioned of depression and sometimes anxiety among the dying. According to Houpt, three concerns underlie the patient's grief: forced dependency, loss of autonomy and sense of competence, and separation from significant others. Each must be dealt with by the patient in order for grief to be resolved. Schulz (1978) addressed the needs of the dying patient, which are related to the concerns identified by Houpt. These needs include: (1) the need to control pain, thought to be the most important; (2) the need to enhance feelings of self-worth and of dignity; and (3) the need for love and affection. Schulz discussed ways in which health professionals can help in meeting these needs and made a strong case for informing patients about their conditions at the same time:

> Just as dignity and feelings of self-worth are enhanced for nonterminal patients by allowing them to perceive themselves as effective agents in their environment, dignity for terminal patients is preserved by allowing them some control in their environment. The tricky part of this is that the terminal patient's environment has traditionally been controlling rather than controlled, and therefore significant changes in the attitudes of medical practitioners are necessary for positive change.

A recent development has been the establishment of hospices, which are oriented toward providing a more positive environment for dying persons. Hospices focus on the prevention of pain, increasing patients' sense of self-worth and autonomy, and expanding family involvement.

Bereavement

Bereavement can be defined as the process of adjusting to another person's death. People report that the most feared and upsetting event in their lives is the loss of a family member, a perception corroborated by research on the stressfulness of different life events. In the period immediately following the death, survivors report somatic distress, feelings of tightness in the throat, choking with shortness of breath, frequent sighing, an empty feeling in the abdomen, and loss of muscular power (Lindemann

1944). Emotional responses to grief include anger, guilt, depression, anxiety and restlessness, and preoccupation with the image of the deceased (Kalish 1976).

The normal grief reaction has been roughly divided into three phases by Schulz (1978). In the first phase, which usually lasts several weeks, the bereaved person feels shock and disbelief. This numbness serves as a barrier against overwhelming pain and sorrow, especially during the first few days after the death, and then may give way to extended periods of crying. The bereaved must also confront anxiety and fears of falling apart, which are often coped with through increased use of alcohol and tranquilizers and an increased emphasis on keeping busy. During the intermediate phase, the bereaved must face living from day to day without the deceased. Specific behaviors often seen include frequent reviews of different ways in which the bereaved individual could have behaved to make things turn out differently (e.g., "If only I'd made him . . ."). Also seen here are searches for the meaning of the death and reports of looking for the deceased and expecting to see her or him momentarily. This phase lasts until about a year has elapsed since the death. During the second year, termed the recovery phase, the bereaved will often make a conscious decision to pick up the pieces and will interact more socially. Also during this phase, if the bereaved is a widow, she will experience the stigma attached to this status. Former friends may avoid her, and widows report being treated as "freaks."

Although both widows and widowers face a difficult adjustment, Atchley (1980) concluded that widows have the additional disadvantages of less likelihood of remarriage and of worse financial status. Another factor thought to influence adjustment is the suddenness of the death; however, findings are mixed, with some investigators reporting fewer problems among people whose spouse's death was anticipated and others coming to the opposite conclusion (Bettis and Scott 1981). Looking at other variables in a program of research on adaptation to widowhood, Lopata (1979) found that positive adjustment was related to access to social groups and good interpersonal relationships. Personality factors, attitudes, and ethnic status also were important. Interestingly, Lopata found that women tend to "sanctify" their deceased husbands, or in other words, to forget all the bad and remember the good. This process interfered with adjustment when it contributed to lack of social participation.

Morbid grief reactions are similar to normal grief responses but differ in the duration and intensity of the response. Lindemann (1944) noted that those people who later exhibited morbid grief reactions often had seemed emotionally detached from the death for several weeks after its occurrence. This internalization of grief led to an increased incidence of somatic disorders such as ulcerative colitis and to behavior changes such as hostility and self-destructiveness. Of people seeking professional help to cope with grief reactions, Parkes (1972) found that two-thirds expressed severe guilt and self-blame regarding the deceased. Most also reported depression, and many revealed a variety of other psychological and somatic symptoms. Furthermore, within the first 4 years of widowhood, suicide occurs so frequently that it exceeds the number of deaths from all other causes (Payne 1975). These grim facts underscore the need for those experiencing morbid grief reactions to receive professional help.

Not surprisingly, a number of studies have linked bereavement to an increase in somatic disorders and to death from natural causes (Averill and Wisocki 1981). For hundreds of years, certain deaths have been ascribed to a "broken heart," and clinical examples are plentiful. More sophisticated recent research has supported the existence of this phenomenon only among those already ill and among older widowers (Clayton 1979). The mechanism that underlies the relationship between bereavement and mortality has not been identified. Currently, the best-supported theory is the desolation hypothesis, which is based on studies of animals showing that physiological changes occur with prolonged stress (Schulz 1978). Whatever the cause, the bereaved should be urged to pay special attention to their health.

SUMMARY AND CONCLUSIONS

Personality tends to remain stable across the life cycle, with the exception of increasing interiority. The literature on locus of control, self-concept, and sex-role behaviors was summarized to illustrate personality research on aging. In an exploration of the relationship between personality type and adaptation to later adulthood, it was concluded that adaptation is more closely related to personality type than to age itself. The disengagement-activity debate of successful adaptation is now thought to be overly simplistic; either extreme is likely to result in maladaptive coping.

Adaptation of elderly people to institutional living appears better than was originally thought, reflecting the significant adaptive capacities of people even late in life. Nevertheless, more must be done both in research and in practice to decrease the stress of relocation and to find alternatives to institutionalization.

Research on retirement has revealed generally positive attitudes toward it, with most workers retiring as soon as they are financially able. Successful coping with retirement has been linked to a variety of personal and situational characteristics.

Marriage can serve as a buffer between elderly couples and many stresses of aging. Unfortunately, after age 65 only 40% of women and 80% of men are still married. For those with living spouses, marital satisfaction is very important in overall life satisfaction. The adult children of the elderly do not neglect their parents; children remain important to parents, and parents to children, across the life cycle.

In recent years there has been a rapid growth of research interest in psychosocial aspects of dying, from the perspectives of the dying themselves, of those left to grieve, and of health professionals. The pervasive fear and denial of death among people in Western culture significantly affects relationships among the dying, their health care professionals, and their families. Research on the dying person has included psychological phases of the dying process and specific concerns and needs of the patient. Similarly, stages of grief have been identified among the bereaved, as have characteristics that affect the mourning process. There is an increased vulnerability to suicide, disease, and death from natural causes among the bereaved.

BIBLIOGRAPHY

Abramowitz, C. F. "Blaming The Mother: An Experimental Investigation of Sex Role Bias in Countertransference." *Psychology of Women Quarterly* 2 (1977):23–24.

Ackerman, N. J. "The Family with Adolescents." In *The Family Life Cycle*, edited by E. A. Carter and M. McGoldrick. New York: Gardner Press, 1980.

Aiken, L. *Later Life*. Philadelphia: W. B. Saunders Co., 1978.

Aller, F. A. "Role of Self-Concept in Student Marital Adjustment." *Family Life Co-ordinator* 11 (1962):43–45.

Alpert, J. L., and Richardson, M. S. "Parenting." In *Aging in the 1980s: Psychological Issues*, edited by L. W. Poon. Washington, D.C.: American Psychological Association, 1980.

American Psychiatric Association. *Diagnostic and Statistical Manual of Mental Disorders*. Washington, D.C.: American Psychiatric Association, 1980.

Amin, M. M. "Drug Treatment of Insomnia in Old Age." *Psychopharmacology Bulletin* 12 (1976):52–55.

Anderson, L., and Burdman, G. D. "Gerontological Interest and Opinions of Health Care Providers." *Educational Gerontology* 6 (1981):251–263.

Arenberg, D. "Concept Problem Solving in Young and Old Adults." *Journal of Gerontology* 23 (1968):279–282.

Arenberg, D., and Robertson-Tchabo, E. A. "Learning and Aging." In *The Handbook of the Psychology of Aging*, edited by J. E. Birren and K. W. Schaie. New York: Van Nostrand Reinhold, 1977.

Atchley, R. C. *The Social Forces in Later Life*. Belmont, Calif.: Wadsworth, 1980.

Atchley, R. C., and Miller, S. J. "Older People and Their Families." *Annual Review of Gerontology and Geriatrics* 1 (1980):337–369.

Averill, J. R., and Wisocki, P. A. "Some Observations on Behavioral Approaches to the Treatment of Grief Among Elderly." In *Behavior Therapy in Terminal Care: A Humanistic Approach*, edited by H. Sobel. Cambridge, Mass.: Ballinger, 1981.

Babikian, H. M. "Abortion." In *The Comprehensive Textbook of Psychiatry/II*, edited by A. M. Freedman, H. I. Kaplan, and B. J. Sadock. Baltimore: Williams and Wilkins, 1975.

Bachtold, L. M. "Similarities in Personality Profiles of College and Career Women." *Psychological Reports* 33 (1973):429–430.

Ballinger, C. B. "The Menopause and Its Syndromes." In *Modern Perspectives in the Psychiatry of Middle Age*, edited by J. G. Howells. New York: Brunner/Mazel, 1981.

Baltes, P. B., and Labouvie, G. V. "Adult Development of Intellectual Performance: Description, Explanation, and Modification." In *Psychology of Adult Development and Aging,* edited by C. Eisdorfer and M. P. Lawton. Washington, D.C.: American Psychological Association, 1973.

Barry, W. A. "Marriage Research and Conflict: An Integrative Review." *Psychological Bulletin* 73, 1 (1970):41–54.

Bart, P. B. "Depression in Middle Aged Women." In *Women in Sexist Society,* edited by V. Garnick and B. K. Moran. New York: Basic Books, 1971.

Bengtson, V. L., Kasschau, P. L., and Ragan, P. K. "The Impact of Social Structure on Aged Individuals." In *The Handbook of the Psychology of Aging,* edited by J. E. Birren and K. W. Schaie. New York: Van Nostrand Reinhold, 1977.

Bernard, J. *The Future of Marriage.* New York: World, 1973.

Bettis, S. K., and Scott, F. G. "Bereavement and Grief." *Annual Review of Gerontology and Geriatrics* 2 (1981):145–159.

Bieliauskas, L. A. *Stress and Its Relationship to Health and Illness.* Boulder, Colo.: Westview Press, 1981.

Billingham, K. A. *Developmental Psychology for the Health Professions: Part I — Prenatal Through Adolescent Development.* Boulder, Colo.: Westview Press, 1981.

Bird, C. *The Two-Paycheck Marriage.* New York: Rawson, Wade Publishers, 1979.

Birnbaum, J. A. "Life Patterns and Self-Esteem in Gifted Family Oriented and Career Committed Women." In *Women and Achievement,* edited by M.T.S. Mednick, S. S. Tangri, and L. W. Hoffmon. New York: John Wiley & Sons, 1975.

Birren, J. E., and Botwinick, J. "Speed of Response as a Function of Perceptual Difficulty and Age." *Journal of Gerontology* 10 (1955):433–436.

Birren, J. E., and Schaie, K. W. (Eds.). *The Handbook of the Psychology of Aging.* New York: Van Nostrand Reinhold, 1977.

Birren, J. E., Woods, A. M., and Williams, M. V. "Behavioral Slowing With Age: Causes, Organization, and Consequences." In *Aging in the 1980s: Psychological Issues,* edited by L. W. Poon. Washington, D.C.: American Psychological Association, 1980.

Bischoff, L. J. *Adult Psychology.* New York: Harper & Row, 1976.

Blanchette, P. A. "Medical Students and Geriatrics." In *Perspectives on Geriatric Medicine.* Washington, D.C.: U.S. Department of Health and Human Services, 1980.

Blazer, D. G. "The Epidemiology of Mental Illness in Late Life." In *Handbook of Geriatric Psychiatry,* edited by E. W. Busse and D. G. Blazer. New York: Van Nostrand Reinhold, 1980.

Block, J. *Lives Through Time.* Berkeley, Calif.: Bancroft, 1971.

Bohannan, P. "Divorce." In *The Comprehensive Textbook of Psychiatry/II,* edited by A. M. Freedman, H. I. Kaplan, and B. J. Sadock. Baltimore: Williams and Wilkins, 1975.

Bohannon, P., and Erickson, R. "Stepping In." *Psychology Today* 11, 8 (1978):53–54, 59.

Botwinick, J. *Cognitive Processes in Maturity and Old Age.* New York: Springer, 1967.

————. "Intellectual Abilities." In *The Handbook of the Psychology of Aging,* edited by J. E. Birren and K. W. Schaie. New York: Van Nostrand Reinhold, 1977.

_____ . *Aging and Behavior.* New York: Springer, 1978.

Bourestom, N., and Pastalan, L. "The Effects of Relocation on the Elderly: A Reply to Borup, J. H., Gallego, D. T., and Hefferman, P. G." *Gerontologist* 21 (1981):4-7.

Boyd, J. H., and Weissman, M. M. "The Epidemiology of Psychiatric Disorders of Middle Age: Depression, Alcoholism, and Suicide." In *Modern Perspectives in the Psychiatry of Middle Age,* edited by J. G. Howells. New York: Brunner/Mazel, 1981.

Brimm, O. G. "Theories of the Male Midlife Crisis." In *Counseling Adults,* edited by N. Schlossberg. Monterey, Calif.: Brooks/Cole, 1977.

Brody, H. "Hope." *Journal of the American Medical Association* 246 (1981):1411-1412.

Bruchner, R. "Longitudinal Research on the Eye." *Gerontology Clinic* 9 (1967):87-95.

Buhler, C. "The Developmental Structure of Goal Setting in Group and Individual Studies." In *The Course of Human Life,* edited by C. Buhler and F. Massarik. New York: Springer, 1968.

Burgess, E. W., and Wallin, P. *Engagement and Marriage.* Philadelphia: Lippincott, 1953.

Burr, W. R. "Satisfaction with Various Aspects of Marriage over the Life Cycle: A Random Middle-Class Sample." *Journal of Marriage and the Family* 32 (1970): 29-37.

_____ . "Satisfaction with Various Aspects of Marriage over the Life Cycle." *Journal of Marriage and the Family* 38, 3 (1976):29-37.

Burrows, G. D., and Dennerstein, L. "Depression and Suicide in Middle Age." In *Modern Perspectives in the Psychiatry of Middle Age,* edited by J. G. Howells. New York: Brunner/Mazel, 1981.

Busse, E. W., and Blazer, D. "Disorders Related to Biological Functioning." In *Handbook of Geriatric Psychiatry,* edited by E. W. Busse and D. Blazer. New York: Van Nostrand Reinhold, 1980.

Butler, R. N. "Overview on Aging." In *Aging: The Process and the People,* edited by G. Usdin and C. J. Hofling. New York: Brunner/Mazel, 1978.

Caldwell, D., and Mishara, B. L. "Research on Attitudes of Medical Doctors Toward the Dying Patient: A Methodological Problem." *Omega: Journal of Death and Dying* 3 (1972):341-346.

Campbell, A. "The American Way of Mating: Marriage Si; Children Only Maybe." *Psychology Today* 8, 12 (1975):37-43.

Campbell, A., Converse, P. E., and Rodgers, W. L. *The Quality of American Life: Perceptions, Evaluations, and Satisfactions.* New York: Russell Sage, 1976.

Canestrari, R. E., Jr. "Paced and Self-Paced Learning in Young and Elderly Adults." *Journal of Gerontology* 18 (1963):165-168.

Carp, F. M. "Housing and Living Environments of Older People." In *Handbook of Aging and the Social Sciences,* edited by R. H. Binstock and E. Shanas. New York: Van Nostrand Reinhold, 1976.

Carter, E. A., and McGoldrick, M. "The Family Life Cycle and Family Therapy: An Overview." In *The Family Life Cycle,* edited by E. A. Carter and M. McGoldrick. New York: Gardner Press, 1980.

Carter, H., and Glick, P. C. *Marriage and Divorce: A Social and Economic Study.* Cambridge, Mass.: Harvard University Press, 1970.

Cerella, J., Poon, L. W., and Williams, D. M. "Age and the Complexity Hypothesis." In *Aging in the 1980s: Psychological Issues,* edited by L. W. Poon. Washington, D.C.: American Psychological Association, 1980.

Clayton, P. J. "The Sequelae and Nonsequelae of Conjugal Bereavement." *American Journal of Psychiatry* 136 (1979):1530–1534.

Cooper, C. L. "Middle-Aged Men and the Pressure of Work." In *Modern Perspectives in the Psychiatry of Middle Age,* edited by J. G. Howells. New York: Brunner/Mazel, 1981.

Costa, P. T., and McCrae, R. R. "Objective Personality Assessment." In *The Clinical Psychology of Aging,* edited by M. Storandt, I. C. Siegler, and M. F. Elias. New York: Plenum Press, 1978.

Cowart, B. J. "Development of Taste Perception in Humans: Sensitivity and Preference Throughout the Life Span." *Psychological Bulletin* 90 (1981):43–73.

Craik, F.I.M., and Lockhart, R. S. "Levels of Processing: A Framework for Memory Research." *Journal of Verbal Learning and Verbal Behavior* 11 (1972):671–684.

Cumming, E., and Henry, W. R. *Growing Old: The Process of Disengagement.* New York: Basic Books, 1961.

Cutler, B. R., and Dyer, W. G. "Initial Adjustment Processes in Young Married Couples." *Social Forces* 44 (1965):195–201.

Denney, A. W., and Palmer, A. M. "Adult Age Differences on Traditional and Practical Problem-Solving Measures." *Journal of Gerontology* 36 (1981):323–328.

Deutscher, I. "Socialization for Postparental Life." In *Marriage and Family in the Modern World,* edited by R. S. Covan. New York: Thomas Y. Crowell, 1969.

Draheim, B. B., and Ashburn, S. S. "Biophysical and Cognitive Development in Young Adulthood." In *The Process of Human Development: A Holistic Approach;* edited by C. S. Schuster and S. S. Ashburn. Boston: Little, Brown and Company, 1980.

Dunlop, K. H. "Maternal Employment and Child Care." *Professional Psychology* 12, 1 (1981):67–75.

Dyer, E. "Parenthood as Crisis: A Re-Study." *Marriage and Family Living* 25 (1963): 196–201.

Eichorn, D. H. "Adulthood." In *Dimensions of Behavior: The Psychiatric Foundations of Medicine,* edited by G. Balis. Boston: Butterworth Publishers, 1978.

Eisdorfer, C. "Arousal and Performance: Experiments in Verbal Learning and a Tentative Theory." In *Human Aging and Behavior,* edited by G. A. Talland. New York: Academic Press, 1968.

――――. "Paranoia and Schizophrenic Disorders in Later Life." In *Handbook of Geriatric Psychiatry,* edited by E. W. Busse and D. G. Blazer. New York: Van Nostrand Reinhold, 1980.

Eisdorfer, C., Nowlin, J., and Wilkie, F. "Improvement of Learning in the Aged by Modification of Autonomic Nervous System Activity." *Science* 170 (1970):1327–1329.

Erber, J. T. "Age Differences in Recognition Memory." *Journal of Gerontology* 29 (1974):177–181.

Erikson, E. H. *Childhood and Society.* New York: W. W. Norton, 1963.

――――. *Identity: Youth and Crisis.* New York: W. W. Norton, 1968.

――――. (Ed.). *Adulthood.* New York: W. W. Norton, 1976.

Eysenck, M. W. "Age Differences in Incidental Learning." *Developmental Psychology* 10 (1974):936–941.

Fein, R. A. "Men's Entrance into Parenthood." *Family Coordinator* 25 (1976):341–348.

Feldberg, R., and Kohen, J. "Family Life in an Anti-Family Setting: A Critique of Marriage and Divorce." *Family Coordinator* 25 (1976):151–159.

Feldman, H. "The Effects of Children on the Family." In *Family Issues of Employed Women in Europe and America,* edited by A. Michel. Leiden: E. F. Brill, 1971.

Feldman, H., and Feldman, M. "Effect of Parenthood at Three Points in Marriage." Unpublished manuscript, 1977.

Felton, B., and Kahana, E. "Adjustment and Situationally-Bound Locus of Control Among Institutionalized Aged." *Journal of Gerontology* 29 (1974):295–301.

Fox, J. H., Topel, J. L., and Huckman, M. S. "Dementia in the Elderly – A Search for Treatable Illness." *Journal of Gerontology* 30 (1975):557–564.

Fozard, J. L. "The Time for Remembering." In *Aging in the 1980s: Psychological Issues,* edited by L. W. Poon. Washington, D.C.: American Psychological Association, 1980.

Friedman, M., and Rosenman, R. H. *Type A Behavior and Your Heart.* Greenwich, Conn.: Fawcett, 1978.

Fuchs, V. R. *Who Shall Live? Health, Economics, and Social Choice.* New York: Basic Books, 1974.

Giambra, L. M., and Arenberg, D. "Problem Solving, Concept Learning, and Aging." In *Aging in the 1980s: Psychological Issues,* edited by L. W. Poon. Washington, D.C.: American Psychological Association, 1980.

Glaser, B. G., and Strauss, H. L. *Awareness of Dying.* Chicago: Aldine, 1965.

Glick, P. C. "Updating the Life Cycle of the Family." *Journal of Marriage and the Family* 39, 1 (1977):5–13.

Gordon, C., Gaitz, C. M., and Scott, J. "Leisure and Lives: Personal Expressivity Across the Life Span." In *Handbook of Aging and the Social Sciences,* edited by R. H. Binstock and E. Shanas. New York: Van Nostrand Reinhold, 1976.

Gottschalk, L. A. "Psychosomatic Medicine Today: An Overview." *Psychosomatics* 19 (1978):89.

Goudy, W. J., Powers, E. A., Keith, P. M., and Reger, R. A. "Changes in Attitudes Toward Retirement: Evidence from a Panel Study of Older Males." *Journal of Gerontology* 35 (1980):942–948.

Gould, R. L. *Transformations: Growth and Change in Adult Life.* New York: Simon and Schuster, 1978.

Gould, R. L. "The Phases of Adult Life: A Study in Developmental Psychology." *American Journal of Psychiatry* 129, 5 (1972):33–43.

Griew, S., Fellows, B. J., and Howes, R. "Duration of Spiral Aftereffect as a Function of Stimulus Exposure and Age." *Perceptual and Motor Skills* 17 (1963):210.

Gurland, B. J. "The Comparative Frequency of Depression in Various Adult Age Groups." *Journal of Gerontology* 31 (1976):283–292.

Haan, N., and Day, D. "A Longitudinal Study of Change and Sameness in Personality Development, Adolescence to Later Adulthood." *International Journal of Aging and Human Development* 5 (1974):11–39.

Hachinski, V. C., Lassen, N. A., and Marshall, J. "Multi-infarct Dementia: A Cause of

Mental Deterioration in the Elderly." *Lancet* 11 (1974):207–209.

Harkins, E. "Effects of Empty-Nest Transition on Self Report of Psychological and Physical Well-Being." *Journal of Marriage and the Family* 40, 3 (1978):549–556.

Harkins, E. B., and House, J. S. "Effects of Empty-Nest Transition on Self Report of Psychological and Physical Well-Being." *Gerontologist* 15 (1975):43.

Harkins, S. W., and Warner, M. H. "Age and Pain." *Annual Review of Gerontology* 1 (1980):121–131.

Harris, L., and Associates. *The Myth and Reality of Aging in America.* Washington, D.C.: National Council on the Aging, 1975.

Hartley, J. T., Harker, J. O., and Walsh, D. A. "Contemporary Issues and New Directions in Adult Development of Learning and Memory." In *Aging in the 1980s: Psychological Issues,* edited by L. W. Poon. Washington, D.C.: American Psychological Association, 1980.

Haug, M. R. "Age and Medical Care Utilization Patterns." *Journal of Gerontology* 36 (1981):103–111.

Havighurst, R. J. "Body, Self, and Society." *Sociology and Social Research* 49 (1965):261–267.

_____. *Developmental Tasks and Education.* New York: David McKay, 1972.

Henker, F. O. "Male Climacteric." In *Modern Perspectives in the Psychiatry of Middle Age,* edited by J. G. Howells. New York: Brunner/Mazel, 1981.

Herman, M. H., and Sedlacek, W. E. "Sexist Attitudes Among Male University Students." *Journal of College Student Personnel* 14 (1973):544–548.

Hickey, T. *Health and Aging.* Monterey, Calif.: Brooks/Cole, 1980.

Hinton, J. *Dying.* Baltimore: Penguin Books, 1967.

Hobbs, D., and Cole, S. "Transition to Parenthood: A Decade of Replication." *Journal of Marriage and the Family* 38, 4 (1976):723–731.

Hobbs, D., and Wimbish, J. "Transition to Parenthood by Black Couples." *Journal of Marriage and the Family* 39, 4 (1977):677–689.

Hoffman, L. W. "Maternal Employment: 1979." *American Psychologist* 34, 10 (1979):859–865.

Holmes, T. H., and Rahe, R. H. "The Social Readjustment Rating Scale." *Journal of Psychosomatic Research* 11 (1967):213–218.

Holtzman, J. M., Beck, J. D., and Ettinger, R. L. "Cognitive Knowledge and Attitudes Toward the Aged of Dental and Medical Students." *Educational Gerontology* 6 (1981):195–207.

Horn, J. C. "Psychometric Studies of Aging and Intelligence." In *Aging (Vol. 2): Genesis and Treatment of Psychologic Disorders in the Elderly,* edited by S. Gershon and A. Raskin. New York: Raven Press, 1975.

Horn, J. L., and Cattell, R. B. "Age Differences in Primary Mental Ability Factors." *Journal of Gerontology* 21 (1966):210–220.

Houpt, J. L. "Death, Dying, and the Family." In *Psychiatry for the Primary Care Physician,* edited by A. M. Freedman, R. L. Sack, and P. A. Berger. Baltimore: Williams and Wilkins, 1979.

Hoyer, W. J., Rebok, G. W., and Sved, S. M. "Effects of Varying Irrelevant Information on Adult Age Differences in Problem-Solving." *Journal of Gerontology* 14 (1979):553–560.

Hulicka, I. M. "Age Differences in Retention as a Function of Interference." *Journal of Gerontology* 22 (1967):180–184.

Hultsch, D. F. "Learning to Learn in Adulthood." *Journal of Gerontology* 29 (1974): 302–308.

Hunt, B., and Hunt, M. *Prime Time*. New York: Dell, 1974.

Hurlock, E. B. *Developmental Psychology: A Life Span Approach*. New York: McGraw-Hill, 1980.

Huston-Stein, A., and Higgins-Trenk, A. "Development of Females from Childhood Through Adulthood: Career and Feminine Role Orientations." In *Life Span Development and Behavior, Vol. 1*, edited by P. B. Baltes. New York: Academic Press, 1978.

Huyck, M. H. "Sex, Gender, and Aging." Paper presented at the 29th Annual Meeting of the Gerontological Society, New York, October 1976.

Hyde, J. S., and Rosenberg, B. G. *Half the Human Experience: The Psychology of Women*. Lexington, Mass.: D. C. Heath and Company, 1976.

Institute of Medicine. *Aging and Medical Education*. Washington, D.C.: National Academy of Sciences, 1978.

Jackson, J. J. "Epidemiological Aspects of Mental Illness Among Aged Black Women and Men." *Journal of Minority Aging* 4 (1979):76–87.

Jacques, J. M., and Chason, K. J. "Cohabitation: Its Impact on Marital Success." *Family Coordinator* 28, 1 (1979):35–39.

Jung, C. G. "The Steps in Life." In *The Collected Works of C. G. Jung, Vol. 8*. New York: Julian Press, 1960.

Kahn, E., and Fisher, C. "The Sleep Characteristics of the Normal Aged Male." *Journal of Nervous and Mental Disease* 148 (1969):477–494.

Kahn, R. L. "The Mental Health System and the Future Aged." *Gerontologist* 15 (1975):24–31.

Kalish, R. A. "Death and Dying in a Social Context." In *Handbook of Aging and the Social Sciences*, edited by R. H. Binstock and E. Shanas. New York: Van Nostrand Reinhold, 1976.

Kalish, R. A., and Knudston, F. W. "Attachment Versus Disengagement: A Life Span Conceptualization." *Human Development* 19 (1976):171–181.

Kart, C. S. "In the Matter of Earle Spring: Some Thoughts on One Court's Approach to Senility." *Gerontologist* 21 (1981):417–423.

Kaslow, F. W. "Divorce and Divorce Therapy." In *Handbook of Family Therapy*, edited by A. Gurman and D. Kniskern. New York: Brunner/Mazel, 1981.

Kastenbaum, R., and Aisenberg, R. *The Psychology of Death*. New York: Springer, 1972.

Kay, D.W.K. "Epidemiological Aspects of Organic Brain Disease in the Aged." In *Aging and the Brain*, edited by C. M. Gaitz. New York: Plenum Press, 1972.

Kelly, E. L. "Consistency of the Adult Personality." *American Psychologist* 10 (1955):659–681.

Kelly, J. R. "Work and Leisure: A Simplified Paradigm." *Journal of Leisure Research* 4, 1 (1972):50–62.

Kieren, D., Henton, J., and Morotz, R. *Hers and His*. Hinsdale, Ill.: Dryden, 1975.

Kimmel, D. C. *Adulthood and Aging*. New York: John Wiley & Sons, 1980.

Knudtson, F. W. "Life Span Attachment: Complexities, Questions, Considerations." *Human Development* 19 (1976):182–196.

Kolodny, R. C., Masters, W. H., and Johnson, V. E. *Textbook of Sexual Medicine.* Boston: Little, Brown and Company, 1979.

Korchin, S. J., and Basowitz, H. "The Judgment of Ambiguous Stimuli as an Index of Cognitive Functioning in Aging." *Journal of Personality* 25 (1956):81–95.

Kovar, M. G. "Elderly People: The Population 65 Years and Over." In *Health in the United States 1976–1977.* Washington, D.C.: U.S. Department of Health, Education, and Welfare, NIH Pub. No. 77-1232, 1977.

Kramer, M., Taube, C. A., and Redick, R. W. "Patterns of Use of Psychiatric Facilities by the Aged: Past, Present, and Future." In *The Psychology of Adult Development and Aging,* edited by C. Eisdorfer and M. P. Lawton. Washington, D.C.: American Psychological Association, 1973.

Kreps, J. M., and Leaper, R. J. "Home Work, Market Work, and the Allocation of Time." In *Women in the American Economy: A Look to the 1980's,* edited by J. M. Kreps. Englewood Cliffs, N.J.: Prentice-Hall, 1976.

Kubler-Ross, E. *On Death and Dying.* New York: Macmillan, 1969.

Kuhlen, R. G. "Developmental Changes in Motivation During the Adult Years." In *Relations of Development and Aging,* edited by J. E. Birren. Springfield, Ill.: Charles C. Thomas, 1964.

Kuypers, J. A. "Internal-External Locus of Control, Ego Functioning, and Personality Characteristics in Old Age." *Gerontologist* 12 (1972):168–173.

Labouvie-Vief, G., and Gonda, J. N. "Cognitive Strategy Training and Intellectual Performance in the Elderly." *Journal of Gerontology* 31 (1976):327–332.

Larson, R. "Thirty Years of Research on the Subjective Well-Being of Older Americans." *Journal of Gerontology* 33 (1978):109–129.

Lasswell, M. E. "Is There a Best Age to Marry? An Interpretation." *Family Coordinator* 23, 3 (1974):237–242.

Laurence, M. W. "A Developmental Look at the Usefulness of List Categorization as an Aid to Free Recall." *Canadian Journal of Psychology* 21 (1967):153–165.

Layton, B., and Siegler, I. "Mid-Life: Must It Be a Crisis?" Paper presented at the Annual Meeting of the Gerontological Society, Dallas, 1978.

Lee, G. R. "Marriage and Morale in Later Life." *Journal of Marriage and the Family* 40 (1978):131–139.

Leech, S., and Witte, K. L. "Paired-Associate Learning in Elderly Adults as Related to Pacing and Incentive Conditions." *Developmental Psychology* 5 (1971):180–186.

LeMaster, E. E. "Parenthood as Crisis." *Marriage and Family Living* 19 (1957): 352–355.

Levinson, D. J. "The Mid-Life Transition: A Period in Adult Psychosocial Development." *Psychiatry* 40 (1977):99–112.

————. *The Seasons of a Man's Life.* New York: Alfred A. Knopf, 1978.

Levinson, D. J., Darrow, C. N., Klein, E. B., Levinson, M. G., and McKee, B. "Periods in the Adult Development of Men: Ages 18 to 45." In *Counseling Adults,* edited by N. K. Schlossberg and A. D. Entine. Monterey, Calif.: Brooks/Cole, 1977.

Lewis, C., and Lewis, M. "The Potential Impact of Sexual Equality on Health." *New England Journal of Medicine* 297, 11 (1977):863–869.

Libow, L. S. "Pseudo-Senility: Acute and Reversible Organic Brain Syndromes." *Journal of the American Geriatric Society* 21 (1973):112–120.

Lieberman, M. A. "Adaptive Processes in Later Life." In *Lifespan Developmental Psychology: Normative Life Crises*, edited by N. Datan and L. Ginsberg. New York: Academic Press, 1975.

Lief, H. I., and Fox, R. C. "Training for Detached Concern in Medical Students." In *The Psychological Basis of Medical Practice*, edited by H. I. Lief and N. R. Lief. New York: Harper & Row, 1963.

Lindemann, E. "Symptomatology and Management of Acute Grief." *American Journal of Psychiatry* 101 (1944):141–148.

Livson, F. B. "Coming Together in the Middle Years: A Longitudinal Study of Sex Role Convergence." Paper presented at the 29th Annual Meeting of the Gerontological Society, New York, October 1976.

_____. "Patterns of Personality Development in Middle-Aged Women: A Longitudinal Study." *International Journal of Aging and Human Development* 7, 2 (1976):107–115.

Lopata, H. Z. *Occupation: Housewife.* London: Oxford University Press, 1971.

_____. *Widowhood in an American City.* Cambridge, Mass.: Schenkman Publishing Company, 1973.

_____. "Couple Companionate Relationships in Marriage and Widowhood." In *Old Family/New Family*, edited by N. G. Molbin. New York: Van Nostrand Reinhold, 1975.

_____. "Widowhood and Husband Sanctification." In *Death and Dying: Theory/Research/Practice*, edited by L. A. Bugen. Dubuque, Iowa: William C. Brown, 1979.

Lowenthal, M. F., and Chiriboga, D. "Transition to the Empty-Nest: Crisis, Challenge, or Relief?" *Archives of General Psychiatry* 28 (1972):8–14.

Lowenthal, M. F., and Havens, C. "Interaction and Adaptation: Intimacy as a Critical Variable." *American Sociological Review* 33 (1968):20–31.

Lowenthal, M. F., Thurnher, M., Chiriboga, D., and Associates. *Four Stages of Life: A Comparative Study of Women and Men Facing Transitions.* San Francisco: Jossey-Bass, 1975.

Lutsky, N. S. "Attitudes Toward Old Age and Elderly Persons." *Annual Review of Gerontology and Geriatrics* 1 (1980):287–336.

McCullough, P. "Launching Children and Moving On." In *The Family Life Cycle*, edited by E. A. Carter and M. McGoldrick. New York: Gardner Press, 1980.

McKain, W. C. *Retirement Marriage.* Storrs: University of Connecticut Agriculture Experiment Station, 1969.

McKenzie, S. C. *Aging and Old Age.* Glenview, Ill.: Scott, Foresman and Company, 1980.

Marsh, G. "Perceptual Changes with Aging." In *Handbook of Geriatric Psychiatry*, edited by E. W. Busse and D. G. Blazer. New York: Van Nostrand Reinhold, 1980.

Masters, W. H., and Johnson, V. E. *Human Sexual Response.* Boston: Little, Brown and Company, 1966.

Matarazzo, J. D. *Wechsler's Measurement and Appraisal of Adult Intelligence.* New

York: Oxford University Press, 1972.

Melzack, R., and Dennis, S. G. "Neurophysiological Foundations of Pain." In *The Psychology of Pain*, edited by R. A. Sternbach. New York: Raven Press, 1978.

Meyer, P. H. "Between Families: The Unattached Adult." In *The Family Life Cycle*, edited by E. A. Carter and M. McGoldrick. New York: Gardner Press, 1980.

Minter, R. E., and Kimball, C. P. "Life Events, Personality Traits, and Illness." In *Handbook of Stress and Anxiety*, edited by I. C. Kutash, L. B. Schlesinger, and Associates. San Francisco: Jossey-Bass, 1980.

Mintz, J., Steuer, J., and Jarvik, L. "Psychotherapy with Depressed Elderly Patients." *Journal of Consulting and Clinical Psychology* 49 (1981):542–548.

Mirkin, P. M., and Meyer, R. E. "Alcoholism in Middle Age." In *Modern Perspectives in the Psychiatry of Middle Age*, edited by J. G. Howells. New York: Brunner/Mazel, 1981.

Mischel, W. *Personality and Assessment*. New York: John Wiley & Sons, 1968.

Monge, R. H. "Studies of the Self-Concept from Adolescence Through Old Age." *Experimental Aging Research* 1 (1975):281–291.

Moos, R. H. "Coping with the Crisis of Physical Illness." In *Psychiatry for the Primary Care Physician*, edited by A. M. Freedman, R. L. Sack, and P. A. Berger. Baltimore: Williams and Wilkins, 1979.

Mossey, J. M., Havens, B., Roos, N. P., and Shapiro, E. "The Manitoba Longitudinal Study on Aging: Description and Methods." *Gerontologist* 21 (1981):551–558.

Mourad, L. A. "Biophysical Development During Middlescence." In *The Process of Human Development: A Holistic Approach*, edited by C. S. Schuster and S. S. Ashburn. Boston: Little, Brown and Company, 1980.

Neiswender, M., Birren, J., and Schaie, K. W. "Age in the Experience of Love in Adulthood." Paper presented at the Annual Meeting of the American Psychological Association, Chicago, 1975.

Neugarten, B. L. "Adult Personality: Towards a Psychology of the Life Cycle." In *Middle Age and Aging*, edited by B. L. Neugarten. Chicago: University of Chicago Press, 1968.

_____ . "The Roles We Play." In *The Quality of Life: The Middle Years*, edited by the American Medical Association. Acton, Mass.: Publishing Sciences Group, 1974.

_____ . "The Future and the Young-Old." *Gerontologist* 15 (1975):4–9.

_____ . "Personality and Aging." In *The Handbook of the Psychology of Aging*, edited by J. E. Birren and K. W. Schaie. New York: Van Nostrand Reinhold, 1977.

_____ . "Time, Age, and the Life Cycle." *American Journal of Psychiatry* 136, 7 (1979):887–894.

Neugarten, B. L., and Associates. *Personality in Middle and Late Life: Empirical Studies*. New York: Atherton Press, 1964.

Neugarten, B. L., and Datan, N. "The Middle Years." In *American Handbook of Psychiatry*, edited by S. Arieti. New York: Basic Books, 1974.

Neugarten, B. L., Havighurst, R. J., and Tobin, S. S. "Personality and Patterns of Aging." In *Middle Age and Aging: A Reader in Social Psychology*, edited by B. L. Neugarten. Chicago: University of Chicago Press, 1968.

Neugarten, B. L., Wood, V., Kraines, R. J., and Loomis, B. "Women's Attitudes

Towards the Menopause." In *Middle Age and Aging: A Reader in Social Psychology*, edited by B. L. Neugarten. Chicago: University of Chicago Press, 1968.

Nuttbrock, L., and Kosberg, J. I. "Images of the Physician and Help-Seeking Behavior of the Elderly: A Multivariate Assessment." *Journal of Gerontology* 35 (1980):241–248.

Nydegger, C. "Middle Age: Some Early Returns—A Commentary." *International Journal of Aging and Human Development* 7, 2 (1976):137–141.

Okun, M. A., Siegler, I. C., and George, L. K. "Cautiousness and Verbal Learning in Adulthood." *Journal of Gerontology* 33 (1978):94–97.

Papalia, D. C., and Olds, S. W. *Human Development*. New York: McGraw-Hill, 1981.

Papanek, H. "Men, Women, and Work: Reflections on the Two-Person Career." In *Changing Women in a Changing Society*, edited by J. Huber. Chicago: University of Chicago Press, 1973.

Parkes, C. M. *Bereavement: Studies of Grief in Adult Life*. New York: International Universities Press, 1972.

Parlee, M. B. "The Rhythms in Men's Lives." *Psychology Today* 11, 11 (1978):82–91.

Payne, E. C. "Depression and Suicide." In *Modern Perspectives in the Psychiatry of Old Age*, edited by J. G. Howells. New York: Brunner/Mazel, 1975.

Peck, R. C. "Psychological Developments in the Second Half of Life." In *Middle Age and Aging: A Reader in Social Psychology*, edited by B. L. Neugarten. Chicago: University of Chicago Press, 1968.

Peskin, H. "Multiple Prediction of Adult Psychological Health and Preadolescent and Adolescent Behavior. *Journal of Consulting Psychology* 38 (1972):155–160.

Pfeiffer, E. "Psychotherapy with Elderly Patients." In *Geriatric Psychiatry*, edited by L. Bellak and T. Karasu. New York: Grune and Stratton, 1976.

Pineo, P. "Disenchantment in the Later Years of Marriage." *Marriage and Family Living* 23 (1961):3–11.

Powell, B. "The Empty-Nest, Employment and Psychiatric Symptoms in College-Educated Women." *Psychology of Women Quarterly* 2 (1977):35–43.

Powell, A. H., Eisdorfer, C., and Bogdonoff, M. "Physiologic Response Patterns Observed in a Learning Task." *Archives of General Psychiatry* 10 (1964):192–195.

Powell, D., Buchanan, S., and Milligan, W. "Relationship Between Learning, Performance, and Arousal in Aged Versus Younger VA Patients." Paper presented at the 28th Annual Meeting of the Gerontological Society, Louisville, October 1975.

Quinn, R. P., and Staines, G. L. *The 1977 Quality of Employment Survey*. Ann Arbor: Institute for Social Research, University of Michigan, 1978.

Quinn, R. P., Staines, G., and McCullough, M. *Job Satisfaction: Is There a Trend?* Manpower Research Monograph No. 30. Washington, D.C.: U.S. Department of Labor, 1974.

Ramey, E. "Men's Cycles." *Ms.* (Spring 1972):8ff.

Rapoport, R., and Rapoport, R. *Working Couples*. New York: Harper Colophon Books, 1978.

Raskind, M. A., and Storrie, M. C. "The Organic Mental Disorders." In *Handbook of*

Geriatric Psychiatry, edited by E. W. Busse and D. G. Blazer. New York: Van Nostrand Reinhold, 1980.

Reichard, S., Livson, F., and Peterson, P. G. *Aging and Personality: A Study of 87 Older Men*. New York: John Wiley & Sons, 1962.

Reno, V. P. "Compulsory Retirement Among Newly Entitled Workers: Survey of New Beneficiaries." *Social Security Bulletin* 35 (1972):3–15.

Rich, A. *Of Women Born: Motherhood as Experience and Institution*. New York: W. W. Norton, 1976.

Roberts, C. L., and Lewis, R. A. "The Empty-Nest Syndrome." In *Modern Perspectives in the Psychiatry of Middle Age*, edited by J. G. Howells. New York: Brunner/Mazel, 1981.

Robinson, J. B. "Historical Changes in How People Spend Their Time." In *Family Issues of Employed Women in Europe and America*, edited by A. Michel. Leiden: E. F. Brill, 1971.

Rockstein, M., and Sussman, M. *Biology of Aging*. Belmont, Calif.: Wadsworth, 1979.

Rogers, D. *The Adult Years: An Introduction to Aging*. Englewood Cliffs, N.J.: Prentice-Hall, 1979.

Rogers, R. R. "On Parenting One's Elderly Parents." In *Modern Perspectives in the Psychiatry of Middle Age*, edited by J. G. Howells. New York: Brunner/Mazel, 1981.

Rollins, B., and Galligan, R. "The Developing Child and Marital Satisfaction of Parents." In *Child Influences on Marital and Family Interactions: A Life Span Perspective*, edited by R. Lerner and G. Spanier. New York: Academic Press, 1978.

Rollins, B. C., and Feldman, H. "Marital Satisfaction over the Family Life Cycle." *Journal of Marriage and the Family* 32 (1970):20–28.

Ross, S., and Walters, J. "Perceptions of a Sample of University Men Concerning Women." *Journal of Genetic Psychology* 122 (1973):329–336.

Rotter, J. B. "Generalized Expectancies for Internal Versus External Control of Reinforcement." *Psychological Monographs* 80, 609 (1966): entire issue.

Rubin, L. B. "The Empty-Nest: Beginning or Ending?" In *Competence and Coping During Adulthood*, edited by L. Bond and J. C. Rosen. Hanover, N.H.: University Press of New England, 1980.

Russell, C. "Transition to Parenthood: Problems and Gratifications." *Journal of Marriage and the Family* 36, 2 (1974):294–302.

Sandberg, E. C. "Psychological Aspects of Contraception." In *The Comprehensive Textbook of Psychiatry/II*, edited by A. M. Freedman, H. I. Kaplan, and B. J. Sadock. Baltimore: Williams and Wilkins, 1975.

Schaie, K. W. "A General Model for the Study of Developmental Problems." *Psychological Bulletin* 64 (1965):92–107.

_____. "Quasi-Experimental Research Designs in the Psychology of Aging." In *The Handbook of the Psychology of Aging*, edited by J. E. Birren and K. W. Schaie. New York: Van Nostrand Reinhold, 1977.

Schaie, K. W., and Parham, I. A. "Stability of Adult Personality: Fact or Fable?" *Journal of Personality and Social Psychology* 34 (1976):146–158.

Schemper, T., Voss, S., and Cain, W. S. "Odor Identification in Young and Elderly Persons: Sensory and Cognitive Limitations." *Journal of Gerontology* 36 (1981):446–452.

Schlossberg, N. K. "A Model for Analyzing Human Adaptation to Transition." *Counseling Psychologist* 9, 2 (1981):2–18.

Schonfield, D. "Memory Changes With Age." *Nature* 28 (1965):918.

Schuckit, M. A., and Pastor, P. A. "Alcohol-Related Psychopathology in the Aged." In *Psychopathology of Aging*, edited by O. Kaplan. New York: Academic Press, 1979.

Schulz, R. *The Psychology of Death, Dying, and Bereavement*. Reading, Mass.: Addison-Wesley, 1978.

Schulz, R., and Brenner, G. "Relocation of the Aged: A Review and Theoretical Analysis." *Journal of Gerontology* 32 (1977):323–332.

Schuster, C. S. "The Decision to Be or Not to Be Parents." In *The Process of Human Development: A Holistic Approach*, edited by C. S. Schuster and S. S. Ashburn. Boston: Little, Brown and Company, 1980.

Schuster, C. S., and Ashburn, S. S. *The Process of Human Development: A Holistic Approach*. Boston: Little, Brown and Company, 1980.

Schwartz, A. N., and Kleemeier, R. W. "The Effects of Illness and Age upon Some Aspects of Personality." *Journal of Gerontology* 20 (1965):85–91.

Schwartz, M. A. "Career Strategies of the Never Married." Paper presented at the 71st Annual Meeting of the American Sociological Association, New York, September 1976.

Shanas, E. "The Status of Health Care for the Elderly." In *Health Care of the Elderly: Strategies for Prevention and Intervention*, edited by G. Lesnoff-Caravaglia. New York: Human Sciences Press, 1980.

Shanas, E., and Maddox, G. L. "Aging, Health, and the Organization of Health Resources." In *Handbook of Aging and the Social Sciences*, edited by R. H. Binstock and E. Shanas. New York: Van Nostrand Reinhold, 1976.

Sheehy, G. *Passages*. New York: E. P. Dutton and Co., 1976.

Sherman, F. T. "Clinical Problems in Geriatric Medicine: A Team Approach." *Allied Health and Behavioral Sciences* 2 (1979):1–18.

Siegel, J. S. "Recent and Prospective Demographic Trends for the Elderly Population and Some Implications for Health Care." In *Second Conference on the Epidemiology of Aging*, edited by S. Haynes and M. Feinleib. Washington, D.C.: U.S. Department of Health, Education, and Welfare, NIH Pub. No. 80-969, 1980.

Siegler, I. C. "The Psychology of Adult Development and Aging." In *Handbook of Geriatric Psychiatry*, edited by E. W. Busse and D. G. Blazer. New York: Van Nostrand Reinhold, 1980.

Simpson, I. H., and McKinney, J. C. *Social Aspects of Aging*. Durham, N.C.: Duke University Press, 1972.

Sinnott, J. D. "Sex-Role Inconstancy, Biology, and Successful Aging: A Dialectical Model." *Gerontologist* 17 (1977):459–463.

Spence, D., and Lonner, T. "The Empty-Nest: A Transition Within Motherhood." *Family Coordinator* 20 (1971):369–375.

Stein, S., and Shamoian, C. A. "Psychosomatic Disorders in the Middle-Aged." In *Modern Perspectives in the Psychiatry of Middle Age,* edited by J. G. Howells. New York: Brunner/Mazel, 1981.

Stone, V. "Gerontological Nursing." In *Health Care of the Elderly: Strategies for Prevention and Intervention,* edited by G. Lesnoff-Caravaglia. New York: Human Sciences Press, 1980.

Streib, G. F., and Schneider, C. J. *Retirement in American Society: Impact and Process.* Ithaca, N.Y.: Cornell University Press, 1971.

Sullivan, J., and Arms, K. G. "Working Women Today and Tomorrow." In *Modern Perspectives in the Psychiatry of Middle Age,* edited by J. G. Howells. New York: Brunner/Mazel,1981.

Super, P. E. *The Psychology of Careers.* New York: Harper & Row, 1957.

Tanner, J. M. *Foetus Into Man: Physical Growth from Conception to Maturity.* London: Open Books, 1978.

Thurnher, M. "Values and Goals in Later Middle Age." Paper presented at the Annual Meeting of the Gerontological Society, Houston, Tex., 1971.

―――― . "Family Confluence, Conflict, and Affect." In *Four Stages of Life,* edited by M. F. Lowenthal and D. Chiriboga. San Francisco: Jossey-Bass, 1975.

Timiras, P. S. *Developmental Physiology and Aging.* New York: Macmillan, 1972.

Tobin, S., and Lieberman, M. A. *A Last Home for the Aged.* San Francisco: Jossey-Bass, 1976.

Treas, J. "The Great American Fertility Debate: Generational Balance and Support of the Aged." *Gerontologist* 21 (1981):98–103.

Troll, L., and Hieger, L. "The Relative Importance of Romantic Love in Three Generations." Paper presented at the meeting of the Gerontological Society, Miami Beach, Fla., 1973.

Troll, L., Miller, S., and Atchley, R. *Families in Later Life.* Belmont, Calif.: Wadsworth, 1979.

Troll, L. E. *Early and Middle Adulthood: The Best Is Yet to Be—Maybe.* Monterey, Calif.: Brooks/Cole, 1975.

Troll, L. E., and Parron, E. M. "Age Changes in Sex Roles amid Changing Sex Roles: The Double Shift." *Annual Review of Gerontology and Geriatrics* 2 (1981):118–143.

U.S. Department of Health, Education, and Welfare, Public Health Service. *Healthy People: The Surgeon General's Report on Health Promotion and Disease Prevention.* Publication No. 79-55071. Washington, D.C.: Government Printing Office, 1979.

Vaillant, G. E. *Adaptation to Life.* Boston: Little, Brown and Company, 1977.

Van Dusen, R. A., and Sheldon, E. B. "The Changing Status of American Women: A Life Cycle Perspective." *American Psychologist* 31 (1976):100–116.

Walsh, D. A., and Thompson, L. W. "Age Differences in Visual Sensory Memory." *Journal of Gerontology* 33 (1978):383–387.

Walsh, F. "The Family in Later Life." In *The Family Life Cycle,* edited by E. A. Carter and M. McGoldrick. New York: Gardner Press, 1980.

Walster, E., and Walster, G. W. *A New Look at Love.* Cambridge, Mass.: Addison-Wesley, 1978.

Weg, R. B. "Physiological Changes That Influence Patient Care." In *Psychosocial Needs of the Aged: A Health Care Perspective*, edited by E. Seymour. Los Angeles: Ethel Percy Andrus Gerontology Center, University of Southern California, 1978.

Weissman, M., and Myers, J. "Depression in the Elderly: Research Directions in Psychopathology, Epidemiology, and Treatment." *Journal of Geriatric Psychiatry* 12 (1979):187–201.

Weissman, M. M., and Paykel, E. S. *The Depressed Woman: A Study of Social Relationships*. Chicago: University of Chicago Press, 1974.

Wells, J. A. "College Women: Seven Years After Graduation: Resurvey of Women Graduates – Class of 1957." Bulletin No. 292. Washington, D.C.: U.S. Department of Labor, Women's Bureau, 1966.

Wells, T. J. "Nursing Committed to the Elderly." In *Current Practice in Gerontological Nursing, Vol. 1*, edited by A. Reinhardt and M. Quinn. St. Louis: C. V. Mosby, 1979.

Westley, W. A., and Epstein, N. B. "Family Structure and Emotional Health: A Case Study Approach." *Marriage and Family Living* 22 (1960):25–27.

Wilensky, H. L. "Orderly Careers and Social Participation: The Impact of Work History on Social Integration in the Middle Mass." *American Sociological Review* 26, 4 (1961):521–539.

Willis, S. L., and Baltes, P. B. "Intelligence in Adulthood and Aging: Contemporary Issues." In *Aging in the 1980s: Psychological Issues*, edited by L. W. Poon. Washington, D.C.: American Psychological Association, 1980.

Wilson, S. R., and Wise, L. *The American Citizen: 11 Years After High School*. Palo Alto, Calif.: American Institute for Research, 1975.

Wilson, K. K., Zurcher, L. A., McAdams, D. C., and Curtis, R. L. "Stepfathers and Stepchildren: An Exploratory Analysis from Two National Surveys." *Journal of Marriage and the Family* 37, 3 (1975):526–536.

Wittels, I. "Age and Stimulus Meaningfulness in Paired-Associate Learning." *Journal of Gerontology* 27 (1972):372–375.

Wolman, B. B., and Money, J. *Handbook of Human Sexuality*. Englewood Cliffs, N.J.: Prentice-Hall, 1980.

Woodruff, D. S., and Birren, J. E. "Age Changes and Cohort Differences in Personality." *Developmental Psychology* 6 (1972):252–259.

Zarit, S. H. *Aging and Mental Disorders*. New York: Free Press, 1980.

Zimberg, S. "The Elderly Alcoholic." *Gerontologist* 14 (1975):221–224.

Zung, W.W.K. "Affective Disorders." In *Handbook of Geriatric Psychiatry*, edited by E. W. Busse and D. G. Blazer. New York: Van Nostrand Reinhold, 1980.

INDEX